MW01625835

"John's dedication to his training mirrors his dedication to his work. Week after week, month after month, he finds time in his busy schedule to show up to the gym and out-hustle people a quarter his age!"

—STEFAN CLOUTIER, JOHN'S PERSONAL TRAINER

"In his beautifully written and thought-provoking book, author John A. Brink brilliantly cracks the code to the fountain of youth, with a focus on healthspan rather than lifespan and on giving his readers the power to live young and die old."

—CHERYL ILOV, BESTSELLING AUTHOR, *FOREVER FIT AND FLEXIBLE: FEELING FABULOUS AT FIFTY AND BEYOND*

"We are largely a world of quick fixes and magic makeovers that look pretty good for a very short while. For lasting change, you need to explore the root of the issue. John Brink exemplifies this success in his knowledge and commitment to exercise, diet, and lifestyle. He makes us look at our excuses and poor choices. Senior health is not all about biology or luck. John Brink shows us how to live our very best life. He is a hero to all of us wanting to age gracefully and wonderfully."

—DR. HEATHER M. BROWNE, PSYD, LMFT

"John Brink's zest for being 'forever young' strikes a nerve in all of us. *Living Young, Dying Old* is an enjoyable read that offers a pragmatic and meritorious approach to increasing healthspan."

—DR. STEVE GULLANS, FORMER ASSOCIATE PROFESSOR, HARVARD MEDICAL SCHOOL

"John's journey is a shining example of what can be achieved when we combine a thirst for knowledge with a passion for healthy living. It has been an honour to be part of his life and to see his efforts unfold. His dedication to wellness is a powerful reminder that we all have the power to create positive change in our lives and to strive for a healthier, happier future."

—ERIN SIMPSON, CEO, FINDING YOUR FREEDOM

This book is dedicated to my wife, Sharon,
as well as my two amazing daughters and four
incredible grandchildren.

LIVING YOUNG

DYING OLD

WRITING ASSISTANCE Guy Saddy

ART DIRECTOR Grace LaFrance

COPY EDITOR Pamela Swanigan

PROOFREADER Pamela Swanigan

Published by Brink Media. Prince George, British Columbia.

Pages 89, 90, 96-97 and 98 photos courtesy of David Aboody; pages 91, 93, 94, 99 and 100 photos courtesy of Scott McWalter; page 92 photo courtesy of Kendall Kershaw; pages 95, 103 and front cover photos courtesy of BB Photography; page 104 photo courtesy of Mohinder Basi; page 191 and back cover flap photo courtesy of Selah & Psalms Photography.

Library and Archives Canada Cataloguing in Publication
Brink, John A., 1940– author
Living Young, Dying Old / John A. Brink

ISBN 978-1-7781546-2-1

Printed and bound in Canada by Friesens Corporation.

FOREWORD

BY JASON BOXTART, ND,
AND TRACEY LOTZE, MD, MB.CHB, CCFP

IN THE QUEST FOR ETERNAL YOUTH, humanity has traversed myriad landscapes of science, folklore, and myth, seeking the elusive elixir that promises to bestow everlasting vitality. Yet, as we stand on the threshold of a new era in biomedicine, we find ourselves confronting a profound truth: the fountain of youth lies not in a magical potion, but in the intricate dance between our genes, our environment, and the choices we make each day.

Tracey and I met John years ago as he was beginning his journey towards "living younger and dying older." As a functional-medicine team, I being a naturopathic physician and Tracey a medical physician, we bring differing but synergistic expertise to our practice.

Together, we have witnessed the transformation in mind and body as we battle the challenges of ageing within the intricate web of disease prevention, health maintenance, and performance improvement. John does all this while managing the challenges of running a significant, multifaceted business. I see our job as keeping the franchise player at the top of his game. This goes for all our patients.

The concept of longevity has undergone a profound transformation in recent years, propelled by groundbreaking discoveries in the field of epigenetics. This burgeoning discipline unveils the remarkable capacity of our genes to respond to environmental cues, regulating their activity in ways that can profoundly impact our health and ageing process. Central to this paradigm shift is the recognition that our biologic age—the age of our cells as determined by epigenetic markers such as DNA methylation—may diverge significantly from our chronologic age. This revelation challenges the conventional notion of ageing as an inevitable march towards decline, inviting us to reimagine the possibilities of healthy longevity.

As we embark on this journey into the depths of our molecular biology, we are confronted with a powerful realization: that the choices we make today have the power to shape not only our own destiny but also the destiny of generations to come. We can begin to do this by embracing a lifestyle characterized by mindful nutrition, regular exercise, and stress management. Combining this approach with strategic use of lab investigation to identify and act on modifiable risk factors, we can tip the scales in favour of health, vitality, and longevity.

But perhaps even more importantly, this journey reminds us of the interconnectedness of all life—the intricate web of relationships that bind us to each other and to the world around us. In nurturing our own well-being, we contribute to the health of our communities, our planet, and future generations.

So, dear reader, we invite you to embark on this transformative odyssey with an open heart and a curious mind. We hope that John's story inspires you to not only transform your own health but also pay it forward, as John does here.

JASON BOXTART, ND

TRACEY LOTZE, MD,
MB.CHB, CCFP

FOREWORD

BY DAVID BILSTROM, MD

IT'S WITH PROFOUND ADMIRATION that I introduce John Brink's fourth book, *Living Young, Dying Old.* This book is a powerful call to action, urging you to redefine the rules of your life. It asks you to let go of the myth that physical and mental decline are a natural part of the ageing process.

In conversing with John and in reading this book, I recognize in John a kinship of spirit and purpose with his proactive approach of optimizing healthspan, not just lifespan.

As a quadruple-board–certified MD who has spent 20 years helping chronically ill people reverse autoimmune disease, I can say with certainty that John is the embodiment of what's possible when you take charge of your mind and body.

This book takes you back into John's childhood, marked by adversity and resilience. Born on the cusp of World War II near the border of Germany, John was traumatized in childhood by the harsh realities of war and starvation. After immigrating to Canada in 1965, he carried with him not just the scars of war but a relentless drive to succeed and a deep appreciation for life.

As you read this book, you'll appreciate the way John distills the complexities of topics like personalized medicine and emerging longevity technologies into understandable and actionable knowledge. His ability to offer clarity across a wide range of topics is a testament to the fact that he's living the wisdom he shares.

As you turn these pages, allow yourself to be guided by John's unwavering commitment to "attitude, passion, and work ethic," the powerful combination that has shaped his remarkable trajectory. Throughout this book, John shows us how to shift our focus from merely adding years to our lives to making our years as rich, rewarding, and purposeful as possible. This is a life where we "live young and die old." Thank you, John!

DAVID BILSTROM, MD

INTRODUCTION

SLOWLY, SLOWLY.

One foot in front of the other. Deep breaths, keep moving. Almost there. Slowly, keep moving. It'll pass. I know it'll pass.

Gasping for breath, I made my way unsteadily to the departure gate, stopping every few metres to gather my strength. The pain was getting worse. By now, it was searing, vibrating, a torment that pulsed through the left side of my body. I almost passed out, but somehow I managed to stay on my feet.

Inch by inch, I trudged forward, determined to make my regular flight from Vancouver International Airport to Prince George—the city in central B.C. where I'd established several successful businesses and much of my life. Normally the walk from Gate A to Gate C at Vancouver International Airport was a five-minute stroll. This time it took me more than 20 minutes.

The pain had come on quickly, and out of nowhere. One Saturday in the spring of 2008, I began experiencing a sharp throbbing in my left lower abdomen. At first I thought it might be a reaction to something I'd eaten: the night before I had been out for dinner with my wife, Sharon, so food poisoning wasn't out of the question. But as the day wore on, my symptoms became more intense.

By Sunday, the pain was so extreme that I literally couldn't get out of bed. And yet, stupidly perhaps, the following morning I steeled myself and got ready to do my weekly commute, intent on catching my usual 5 a.m. flight from Vancouver Island back to Prince George. When I finally made it onto the plane, I collapsed into my seat. But I could barely sit without screaming.

The *pain.*

In all my life, I'd never felt anything like this. By almost any measure, I can tolerate an unbelievable amount of discomfort, and I've had to do so on more than a few occasions. But this concerned me. No, it scared me: this went beyond the worst pain I'd ever experienced in my life. And that is saying something. One time in particular stands out.

On a cold and wintry Friday evening many years ago, when I was still a young man, I was sitting at my desk running numbers when one of my employees came in. "John," he said, "we have a problem with the cyclone. It's plugged." The cyclone is the heart of a sawmill's dust collection system; it runs constantly to clear sawdust and shavings from the equipment, so it's a critical part of any lumber-manufacturing facility. And if it stops working, the mill has to be shut down.

I went outside to check things out. As the owner of many diverse businesses—today, they range from logistics to real-estate development—I've always operated under the assumption that no task is below me. My primary business, however, is forestry. More specifically, it's the production of what's called "secondary manufactured wood products." In a nutshell, we fashion wood studs out of small, basically unusable lengths of lumber and join them together to make a product that is stronger than any "normal" stud cut from a perfect tree. It is an innovative process that, in Canada, I pioneered. As a result, I have literally had my hands on every bolt and screw that was used to create my original manufacturing plant in the first place. I know how to operate and fix every piece of machinery in my entire mill. I'm as hands-on as you can be. And so of course I headed outside to see what I could do.

A light snow was falling, the flakes illuminated by the yard lights. A couple of our guys were working on the cyclone, trying to clear the jam, but whatever they were doing wasn't working. I looked at my watch: we'd been down for about half an hour by this time, and I wanted things to be up and running smoothly for the overnight shift.

I climbed the ladder to the opening, about 10 feet off the ground, opened the cyclone door, and peered inside. I felt around a bit: there was a stick blocking the downward path of the wood shavings. I reached in to try and pull the stick out.

As I did, someone inside the mill turned on the blower.

Fire shot out of the cyclone with a full, scorching blast. I felt the flesh on my face and hands start to melt. "He's on fire! He's on fire!" people were screaming. I quickly realized that my jacket was in flames, and I tried my best to tear it off before sliding down the ladder. I could feel the loose burned skin on my hands sticking to the rails as I descended. When I reached the ground, I rolled around in the snow to put out the remnants of the burning jacket. People were clustered all around me, and as I got up, I told them to get the mill restarted. Only then did I make my way to the office to see how bad my face was. I got my answer when I passed a clerk working in the office. She screamed when she saw me.

I survived, of course, though I still have the burn scars. I was even back at work the next morning. As you'd guess, the pain was excruciating. But although I thought nothing could be worse than what I endured then, it didn't compare to what I was going through on that plane, en route to central British Columbia, my insides on fire.

Finally we landed. At the hospital in Prince George, I was diagnosed with acute diverticulitis, an eruptive gastrointestinal attack that can be fatal if left untreated. By the time I was seen, it had been 48 hours since my symptoms first appeared; I was entering what they call "the danger zone." Emergency surgery was the only option. My colon had ruptured in several places, and toxins were oozing into my body cavity. To save my life, they had removed a 20-centimetre section of my colon. When I woke up, my doctor told me I almost hadn't made it.

The attack was a wake-up call. I realized that to continue along the path I was on—eating poorly, not exercising enough, sacrificing my personal health to maximize the financial health of my businesses—was simply not an option. Over the years, stress had taken a toll. So too had smoking and, for a time, a daily routine that included consuming more alcohol than I should have. When I got back home, I looked at myself in the mirror. I wasn't crazy about what I saw. An old guy, in the initial stages of physical deterioration.

I needed to do something. I needed to change. I needed to make the kind of decisions that could turn around decades of self-neglect. If I continued on this path, I could clearly see the road ahead: years of declining physical and cognitive ability, followed by a too-early death.

This was not for me. This would not be my fate. I wanted to live—to over 100 certainly, but maybe even to 120 years old, a marker that we now know is increasingly within our collective reach. But chronological milestones don't tell the whole truth. Yes, I would do what it took to extend my lifespan. But more importantly, I would strive to extend my healthy years along with it. I wanted *healthy ageing*: to live well, robustly, and in excellent health, my cognitive abilities fully intact. I wanted to be a person who, no matter how old, was an achieving, aspiring, and relevant contributor to the world and his community. I was not interested in slow slippage, that inexorable degradation of mind, body, and spirit that occurs until life's light finally sputters out, like a barely flickering candle succumbing to the lightest breeze.

No, I told myself, *this will not be me*.

And today, as I approach my mid-80s, it's not.

Look around you today, and more and more you'll see women and men defying the expectations of what it means to be an "older person" in the world. Take Noam Chomsky, for example. No matter what you think of his politics, at 95 years old he remains one of the most celebrated, controversial, and influential thinkers on the planet—and he's still weighing in with his trademark gravitas on the big issues of our day, his arguments and mind as sharp as ever. Or Saskatchewan-born Olga Kotelko. By 2014, before she succumbed to an intracranial hemorrhage in her 95th year—just a few days after participating in a track meet—she had amassed 30-plus world records in track and field, a remarkable achievement made even more remarkable when you consider that she began her sports career at the age of 77.

Although former U.S. president Jimmy Carter, 99 years old at the time of this writing, is now in hospice care, he was building homes for the homeless well into his 90s. Award-winning actor Robert Duvall continues to land jobs at 93, despite being of an age where the juicy parts almost always go to much younger actors—because, well, he's just so good.

As all these remarkable people show—and really, there are so many others—it's not "age" that can create barriers to doing fantastic, meaningful things well into your 80s, 90s and beyond. We're coming up to a future where people 100 years old or older, once almost as rare as unicorns, will become an everyday fixture in our culture: the United Nations projects that by 2050, the total number of centenarians in the world will have risen from about 600,000 to nearly 4 million.

This presents us with an opportunity: very soon, we can look forward to a time when many more lives will extend past 100 years. This has the potential to change the world—tapping into the accumulated wisdom and knowledge of people who have a century or more of living under their belts! How could this be anything but amazing?

But to make it amazing, we need to ensure that along with extending our lives, we are also extending our health. And that is what this book is about.

Let me be clear: first, I'm not an expert. I'm not a doctor. I don't have a background in medical research. I don't pretend to have all the answers. If you're looking for an oracle to guide personal decisions centred on your own health, I'm going to suggest you look elsewhere. And there are many places to look.

The topic of human longevity has generated a tsunami of interest, especially in the past few years. In 2023, *Outlive: The Science and Art of Longevity*, written by Canadian physician Peter Attia, rocketed to the top of almost every bestseller list, despite being so densely packed with medical information as to be, in my opinion, almost impenetrable. The popular Netflix documentary series *Live to 100: Secrets of the Blue Zones* followed author and journalist Dan Buettner on a global quest to determine how lifestyle and environment contribute to the extraordinary lifespans regularly observed in five disparate locations around the world; millions of health-conscious viewers went along for the ride.

In Silicon Valley, tech magnates like Bryan Johnson are biohacking their lives and investing millions of dollars in life-extension strategies, and other "buff billionaires" like Jeff Bezos and Peter Thiel are pouring cash into life-extension research companies such as Altos Labs. (Stock options, anyone?) Astonishingly, some biomedical gerontologists are even pursuing strategies designed to basically defeat death—a controversial goal, to be sure. From Stanford in the U.S. to the University of British Columbia's Centre for Longevity, academics and researchers are grappling with the same questions: How can we live longer, healthier lives? Can we all expect to live past 100? And if so, what are the implications?

These are incredibly textured questions. And they're being looked at by women and men who each have decades of research experience, with degrees in fields that run the gamut from economics and public health to neuroscience, gerontology, oncology, and beyond. What, then, can a layman like John Brink bring to this already crowded party?

Frankly, the most I can offer is my natural curiosity and my own life as an example. After almost succumbing to diverticulitis, I completely changed the way I lived. I gave up smoking and alcohol. My diet, which once leaned heavily on red meat and dairy, shifted toward an emphasis on fresh fruit and vegetables. (That said, I'm not a vegetarian, although my wife, Sharon, is.)

At the age of 83, I continue to work long hours on a daily basis, getting up at 5:30 a.m. and rarely making it home until 9:00 p.m. On weekends, I ride horses, dressage-style. I'm currently the oldest competitive bodybuilder in North America. My energy is practically boundless, and my philanthropy was recently recognized by the B.C. government: in 2017 I was awarded the Order of British Columbia, the province's highest honour. Oh, and this isn't my first rodeo: I'm a published author with three other books under my belt. I also have done more than 250 *On the Brink* podcasts, on subjects ranging from business and personal growth to health; currently, we've surpassed over 20 million views on YouTube, and we have a reach that is global.

And I've been a guest on over 150 podcasts from around the world.

Today, I'm in fantastic health—something to which my two doctors, one a traditional physician and the other a naturopathic doctor, will freely attest. That could shift on a dime, of course, and I could drop dead while you're reading this: there are no guarantees. But I'm not looking for guarantees. Rather, I'm looking to make sure that my health never gets in the way of my life—and post-diverticulitis, I can assure you, that's something that I've never allowed.

In this book, we'll look at the history of ageing. We'll seek to understand the kind of health challenges that are loosely grouped as "diseases of ageing," and what is currently being done to stave them off. We'll look at how knowing *who you are*—everything from understanding resting heart rate to knowing your VO2 max scores—can help you make the healthy choices that could pay out in the dividend of a long and vibrant life. We'll look at what we can change and what we can't (at least not easily).

And finally, we'll blue-sky a world where we incorporate many of the exciting discoveries currently being made in the realm of longevity research—and how our healthcare systems might be able to adapt to better serve those whom they are supposed to be serving.

Together, along with millions of people around the globe, we are about to embark on an extraordinary adventure. We are entering uncharted waters, a future where many of us will live until 120 years old—my new goal, by the way. But in this brave new world, we need to make a brave choice: we can live as frail, confused, and disintegrating seniors, or we can remain active and engaged members of society, living full and robust lives, unfettered by the kind of mental and physical deterioration that, until now, has unfortunately often been the hallmark of old age.

It is a future of relevance and living abundantly. It is one in which I hope you'll join me.

Yours in good health,

JOHN A. BRINK

SECTION ONE

THE BACKSTORY

CHAPTER ONE

A HISTORY OF LIVING LONGER

Since before the dawn of recorded history, humankind has sought ways to extend life. From arcane rituals to major organized religions, we've sought to delay or even cheat death. Along the way, we've learned a lot about structuring our world so that we can inhabit it for just a little longer. But have we truly been successful in this quest? And how much snake oil has been sold along the way?

SO HOW FAR BACK CAN WE TRACE OUR OBSESSION WITH LIVING LONGER?

Great kick-off question! As I've said, our interest in life extension can probably be traced back to even before civilization. Most religious and spiritual belief systems that conceive of a world where there is no end—a place where people who die continue to live, at least metaphorically—are likely a direct reaction to fear about our own mortality. That's a bit of a word salad, but I think it's true.

> **O excellent! I love long life better than figs.**
>
> —WILLIAM SHAKESPEARE, *ANTONY AND CLEOPATRA*

Try to imagine that you're living the same life as your ancestors did maybe 10,000 years ago. There was so much that was unknown. A shooting star flies across the night sky. The earth shakes beneath their feet. Herds of animals, once found everywhere, begin dropping dead or moving on. What do you do? With the knowledge you have at hand, how do you make sense of the catastrophic or the inexplicable?

YOU CREATE A WORLD THAT HELPS TO EXPLAIN THINGS?

Correct. You invent reasons for things that happen. To take randomness or chance or coincidence out of the equation, you must concoct a rationale for why things occur. The shooting star? That's a chariot driven by the god of the hunt, whose wrath has been provoked by not paying respect to his greatness. So you kill a stag or sacrifice few dozen villagers, to appease an "entity" that stands in for anything you don't have the tools to explain.

The shaking earth? It's a sleeping giant that lies underneath the mountain, now angry after being awakened. To make sure he rests easy, you kill a stag or sacrifice a few dozen villagers. A tsunami that wipes out thousands? The sea god has been angered, so you appease him by killing a stag or sacrificing a few dozen villagers. Flocks of birds fall from the sky, so it's clear—

I THINK I GET IT.

Of course you do! And so, a collection of myths fills a void where our existing knowledge encounters a dead end.

How does this factor into life extension? Well, if things that afflict us exist beyond our ability to comprehend, then perhaps wonderful things also await us. And they, too, are beyond our ability to comprehend. We create a world where magic rules. This provides comfort, direction, and meaning. In a way, it's a world where anything is possible. Surprises are everywhere. And explanations—and antidotes—abound for all the things that can harm us or shorten our lives.

Underpinning much of this is the search for eternal youth, which, according to many legends, wasn't confined to metaphysics. Like the famous quest of Ponce de Leon, for example.

> **Wanting to return to a youthful state or live forever is a basic, animating human response to the uncertainty of death.**
>
> —JOHN BRINK

I'VE HEARD ABOUT HIM, BUT CAN YOU FILL IN THE BLANKS?

Sure. Juan Ponce de Leon was a Spanish explorer and *conquistador*, the first European to explore Florida, and the subject of perhaps the most famous longevity-quest yarn. Ponce de Leon had heard stories from the local Arawak people about an island called Bimini, which supposedly was home to waters that would reverse the ageing process if you drank from them. Allegedly, he set out to find this mythical spring.

WHY "ALLEGEDLY"? WASN'T HE A REAL PERSON?

Ponce de Leon was definitely a historical figure and, yes, in the early 1500s he did explore *La Florida*, as the area was then called by the Spanish colonialists. But the story of him searching for the mythical Fountain of Youth only arose after his death, when the supposed quest was mentioned in a biography.

There is no evidence that Ponce de Leon searched for the Fountain. He never mentioned it. And obviously, the accounts of such a spring were entirely fictional. But this is how myth and legend are made. And it's not the first time that an anti-ageing fountain or spring figured in the history of longevity.

REALLY? THERE WERE OTHER "FOUNTAINS OF YOUTH"?

Sure, history mentions several. For example, the famed Greek historian Herodotus, who lived back in the 5th century BC, recounted one. This version claimed that the Macrobians, an ancient people from either Africa or India, used to bathe in a certain kind of water, and this kept them young. Here's what Herodotus writes about it in his famous *Histories*:

> *"The Ichthyophagi then in their turn questioned the king concerning the term of life, and diet of his people, and were told that most of them lived to be a hundred and twenty years old, while some even went beyond that age—they ate boiled flesh, and had for their drink*

> *nothing but milk. When the Ichthyophagi showed wonder at the number of the years, he led them to a fountain, wherein when they had washed, they found their flesh all glossy and sleek, as if they had bathed in oil—and a scent came from the spring like that of violets. . . .If the account of this fountain be true, it would be their constant use of the water from it which makes them so long-lived."*

Clearly this was a second-hand version—and, in a way, the first "Blue Zone" reference in history! (More on that later.) But I love the goal: living to 120 years sounds pretty reasonable, I think.

The Herodotus story obviously predates Ponce de Leon. It may have been the first mention of the existence of magical life-extending waters, but there were others. Alexander the Great supposedly crossed the mythical Land of Darkness and discovered a similar spring. And let's not forget the Biblical story of the Pool of Bethesda, where Jesus cured a paralyzed man by dunking him in its waters. Not longevity-related, exactly, but magical nonetheless.

The main point behind all these stories is that the desire to live forever or return to a youthful state is a common human response to the uncertainty that surrounds death. Here's some food for thought, and a bit of paradox: some religions promise an improved state after life is over. Regarding Heaven, our reward for living a good or godly life is eternity in paradise. If that's the case, why bother trying to cheat death? Shouldn't we embrace the end of life, and all be death cultists? It seems to me that this would make more sense.

THAT'S A GOOD POINT.

And a bit off topic. But you're dealing with someone who has the gift of ADHD: with me, digressions and diversions are all part of the package. So let's change gears again. You're aware of the so-called terracotta soldiers, yes?

YOU MEAN THE ONES IN CHINA?

Exactly. They were discovered in 1974, although Chinese historians had reported the existence of the mausoleum centuries earlier. It was basically a tomb to house the earthly remains of Qin Shi Huang, China's first emperor. Like the Egyptian pharaohs, Qin Shi Huang wanted to be surrounded by an army so he could be protected in the afterlife. But there is an irony embedded in this story.

For Qin Shi Huang, his terracotta army may have been, excuse the pun, overkill. According to a BBC report, the Chinese emperor was quite taken with the concept of living forever—or at least for around 10,000 years, which should have given him more than enough time to finish signature infrastructure projects like the Great Wall. But this was a man who believed in possibilities. To stave off death, he regularly took cinnabar. This concoction consisted of wine, honey—all good, so far—and quicksilver, or, as we know it today. . .mercury. In this case, the "cure" wasn't worse than the disease: the cure *was* the disease. Qin Shi Huang likely died of mercury poisoning after being on the planet for just 49 years.

No one is sure who "prescribed" the mercury cure. In a way, though, it was arguably history's first case of snake oil.

> **Let thy food be thy medicine and thy medicine be thy food.**
>
> —HIPPOCRATES

I'VE HEARD THAT TERM BEFORE. BUT WHAT EXACTLY DOES IT MEAN?

> **No disorders have employed so many quacks, as those that have no cure; and no sciences have exercised so many quills, as those that have no certainty.**
>
> —CHARLES CALEB COLTON

Ah, this one is interesting—mainly for how the term became synonymous with fake medicine. This wasn't initially the case. The roots of snake oil stretch back to China. But far from being a health scam, there is evidence that there was a solid basis for its use, just like a lot of traditional Chinese medicines that we perhaps unfairly think of as unconventional or alternative.

As an article from U.S. public broadcaster National Public Radio relates, Chinese immigrants who came to America in the mid-1800s to work on the railroad brought with them oil from the Chinese water snake, a substance rich in omega-3 fatty acids. The railroad workers rubbed the oil on their skin after work to ease joint problems like arthritis and bursitis. If you follow health trends even a little bit, you'll know that omega-3 is an effective anti-inflammatory—so much so that, the story goes, the American railroad workers took notice. They began using it too, and "marveled at the effects."

So snake oil was real medicine—at least in its original form, before the "snake oil salesmen" got hold of it.

WHAT HAPPENED TO GIVE IT SUCH A BAD NAME?

As I said, salespeople became involved. In North America, this period has been referred to as "The Golden Age of Quackery." It was a time when all sorts of ridiculous concoctions were marketed, often as "cure-alls" for pretty much every ailment under the sun.

The sheer number of products was astonishing. A good example of quackery was Texas gardener William Radam's wildly popular "Microbe Killer," a "medicine" that Radam started selling by the jug in 1886. He claimed that his mixture would kill not only the dread disease tuberculosis but "Cure All Diseases"—a remarkable thing, when you consider that its main contents were sulphur, sandalwood, and a bit of red wine to turn it pink. As one naturally assumes, it cured absolutely nothing.

There were others, too. As one website notes, frauds used the introduction of electricity—a modern marvel!—to enhance the marketing of their "cures." One of my favourites? Bloxam's Electric Hair Restorer, circa 1890. A newspaper ad touts that it "Restores grey hair to its natural color, beauty and softness, keeps the head cool, clean and free of dandruff . . .Will not soil the skin or the most delicate head dress." Where does the "electricity" in the Electric Hair Restorer come into play? We have no idea. And we will never know.

Then there were Beecham's Pills. These little miracles, which addressed "all bilious and nervous disorders to which men, women and children are subject," were sold as "the most marvellous antidote yet discovered." Sad to say, they were discontinued—in *1998*. You may have heard of the company that last marketed the pills: SmithKline Beecham, one of the largest pharmaceutical manufacturers in the world.

IT SEEMS ALMOST INCREDIBLE THAT THIS WAS GOING ON.

I should also mention "Pink Pills for Pale People"—yes, seriously. They handily dispatched all of the following, if you were a "pale person," I guess: "Poor and Water Blook [sic], Anemia, Chlorosis or Green Sickness, Dizziness, Palpitation of the Heart, Nervous Headache, Loss of Appetite, Indigestion and Dyspepsia, After-Effects of the Grip, Eruptions and Pimples, Sick Headache, Pale or Sallow Complexion, Swelling of Hands or Feet, General Debility, Depression of Spirits,

Insomnia or Loss of Sleep, General Muscular Weakness, Shortness of Breath on Slight Exertion, Spinal Troubles, Partial Paralysis, Locomotor Ataxia, Chronic or Acute Rheumatism, Sciatica, Neuralgia, Chronic Erysipelas, Catarrh of the Stomach, Nervous Fits, St. Vitus' Dance, Swelled Glands, Scrofula, Fever Sores, Rickets, After-Effects of Acute Diseases such as Fevers, All Female Weakness, Tardy or Irregular Periods, Leucorrhea, Suppression of the Menses, Loss of Vital Forces, Loss of Memory, Ringing in the Ears, Hysteria, etc."

Et cetera, too! It's a miracle. Many of these "cures" had actual money behind their invention and marketing—and, sometimes, misguided scientists or doctors. However, the stuff that was hawked at the travelling medicine shows must have been on a different level entirely.

WHAT ARE "TRAVELLING MEDICINE SHOWS"?

They're just what the name implies: road shows where scam artists would sell "patent medicines" to the masses. The shows were based on a European model called the "mountebank." But the ones in the United States, especially, were full of spectacle, with some of the larger ones featuring performers and entertainers—"fun for the whole family," in fact. Some claim they were almost as popular as travelling circuses, another staple of the 1800s and early 1900s.

BUT SURELY THERE WAS SOME SORT OF OVERSIGHT? RIGHT?

I'm afraid not. In America, these hacks sold their fraudulent products without any significant government regulation until 1906, when the Pure Food and Drug Act was legislated into law. Still, false claims continued to be made until the mid-1900s and beyond.

But remember, quackery's golden age was a time when new scientific knowledge was being grossly misapplied, resulting in some terrible outcomes. The discovery of genetics led to pseudoscience such as phrenology: using the shape and size of a person's head to determine, say, their criminal personality. Social Darwinists abused the popularization of evolutionary theory to create a pecking order of race, which ended up underpinning the Nazi obsession with Aryan supremacy, which in turn led to the Holocaust.

In the wrong hands, science and ideas—and medicine—can do great harm. Even today, we see an abundance of unsupported claims by "health professionals" who stretch the truth or inflate their own expertise to sell a product. In many cases, "follow the money" is a good rule of thumb.

HOW SO?

If someone is selling something along with the medical information they're providing, that should inspire you to take a sober second look at the source's credibility. It's not always a scam, of course, and people need to make a living. But if healthcare or medicinal claims come wrapped in a marketing campaign for a product, it's just common sense to take a closer look before diving in before potentially jeopardizing your health—and giving up your hard-earned dollars.

A good starting place is the "Quack Miranda Warning." You see this on many products of dubious benefit.

I'VE NEVER HEARD OF THIS. WHAT'S A "QUACK MIRANDA WARNING"?

It's a disclaimer, nothing more. It's often written in a much smaller font size than the surrounding material and worded something like this: "*These claims have not been evaluated... This product is not intended to diagnose, treat, cure, or prevent any disease.*" What does this say about the "medical" company and what they're trying to sell you?

In truth, it probably offers them very little legal protection. What it really does, for the consumer, is alert us to the fact that the product has not been subject to medical scrutiny—or at least, not enough to ensure that its use could help and not hurt. It's another bright red flag. Actually, this one's more like a flare.

> **These claims have not been evaluated...This product is not intended to diagnose, treat, cure, or prevent any disease.**
>
> —EXAMPLE OF A "QUACK MIRANDA WARNING"

It would be almost comical if it weren't an ongoing concern. In 2017, for example, the U.S. Food and Drug Administration sent out over a dozen warnings to companies that were claiming to offer "cures" for cancer—without any real evidence to back up their claims, of course. It's fraud.

Frauds, scams and misinformation target people who are at their most vulnerable. They also prey on a very common and worthwhile desire: to continue to live in good health for as long as we possibly can.

But even trying to expose these bad actors can land you in hot water. As we all know, the U.S. is a very litigious society. Case in point: a well-respected academic and gerontologist, S. Jay Olshansky of the School of Public Health at the University of Illinois at Chicago, used to give out yearly "Silver Fleece Awards" to companies who, in the opinion of Olshansky and other experts, were fleecing consumers with medical treatments that amounted to quackery.

In 2002, the first Silver Fleece went to a company called Clustered Water from Olympia, Washington. They were hawking a "nontoxic water solution" that they claimed would reverse the ageing process. Sound familiar?

PONCE DE LEON! THE FOUNTAIN OF YOUTH, RIGHT?

Exactly. Sadly, though, the Silver Fleece Awards no longer are a thing.

WHY DID THEY STOP?

Olshansky was on the receiving end of a defamation lawsuit brought against him by another company in 2005. He countersued. Eventually both parties agreed to drop their respective lawsuits. So even when you're doing something that's in the public interest, there are ways to block the kind of discussions that we need to have.

And oh man, do we need to have those discussions today.

WHY DO YOU SAY THAT? WHAT'S HAPPENED RECENTLY?

Turn on the news, and you'll get an idea. In my opinion, the most egregious quackery I've ever seen took place during the Covid-19 pandemic. And some of those claims came from people who should have known better. Donald Trump, for example, was a disseminator of quackery. The amount of b.s. that this guy slung on a regular basis was just astonishing.

EXAMPLES, PLEASE?

Well, he championed hydroxychloroquine, for example. Very early in the pandemic, reporters quizzed Dr. Anthony Fauci, director of the National Institute of Allergy and Infectious Diseases, as to whether there was any merit to a study touting the drug as a potential cure for coronavirus. Fauci unequivocally answered, 'No.' Then, Dr. Donald J. Trump, MD, PhD., stepped up: "May work, may not," he said. "I feel good about it. That's all it is, just a feeling, you know, smart guy."

Throughout the course of the pandemic, this would be the kind of messaging that, if not directly endorsed by the White House, was at least given a hearing. Ivermectin, for example, is an amazing drug, no question about this. The people who invented it were awarded a Nobel prize in 2015. But it is amazing for treating worms in horses, not alleviating Covid-19 symptoms in human beings.

> **May work, may not...I feel good about it. That's all it is, just a feeling, you know, smart guy.**
>
> —FORMER U.S. PRESIDENT DONALD TRUMP, REFLECTING ON THE ABILITY OF HYDROXYCHLOROQUINE TO TREAT COVID-19.

Similarly, the health claims for "convalescent plasma" and drugs like Oleandrin, a favourite of arch Trump supporter and MyPillow founder Mike Lindell, had zero merit. None of these quack treatments worked. In Trump you have a guy who was the most powerful person in the world, and who was supposed to be at the top of the political food chain, spouting and tolerating crackpot theories that led many vulnerable people down a dangerous or even deadly path.

In fact, by 2022, between people refusing to get vaccinated, taking COVID "cures" such as Ivermectin, and other outcomes of crackpot claims, the head of the FDA was calling medical misinformation "the leading cause of death in the United States." And with social media accelerating the spread (researchers have found that on X, for instance, wrong information travels six times faster than correct information), the World Health Organization has declared that we're in an "infodemic."

This is what we're up against in our quest to live longer and healthier lives. But with the right tools, we can move on from junk science and quackery, into a brave and beautiful future.

First, though, we need to take stock of where we're at. We'll do this in Chapter 2.

CHAPTER TWO

THE NUMBERS GAME

Today, there's no shortage of researchers aiming to ensure we live the longest lives we can. But is this the goal we should be pursuing? It's one thing to live a long life. It's quite another to live a long and healthy *life. The first step on this journey is to make sure that the latter goal is in our sights—and to do that we must also establish a "baseline" of health indicators from which we'll chart our progress. To "heal thyself," first you need to know thyself.*

YOU'VE CALLED THIS CHAPTER "THE NUMBERS GAME". WHAT DO YOU MEAN BY THIS?

I'm glad you asked this, but with your permission, I'll give you some background before I explain. Usually when we talk about longevity, we end up discussing life extension. Frankly, humans have succeeded in extending our collective lifespan for a very long time now.

> **It's one thing to live a long life. It's quite another to live a long and *healthy* life.**
>
> —JOHN BRINK

OBVIOUSLY PEOPLE ARE LIVING LONGER THAN THEY USED TO. THAT'S NOT PARTICULARLY REVOLUTIONARY.

Well, yes—and no. First, we need to know that the concept of "life expectancy" is a complex statistical one, involving probability formulas, and generally speaking, a layperson has a pretty vague understanding of how it works. For example, in the Middle Ages, the life expectancy at birth was 33 years on average. According to a 2005 study published in *International Journal of Epidemiology*, this was a significant improvement over the status quo during the Roman Empire's heyday. Back then, Roman life expectancy was about 25 years old.

Not so great, eh? You're barely out of high school when you have to start planning your funeral.

NO KIDDING. THAT'S NOT MUCH TO LOOK FORWARD TO!

But there's always a "but." These stats don't reflect the true nature of how long our ancestors were living. In fact, the study's authors note that if you were lucky to escape dying in childhood—say you made it to

> **A long life may not be good enough, but a good life is long enough.**
>
> —BENJAMIN FRANKLIN, WRITER, SCIENTIST, INVENTOR, STATESMAN, AND POLITICAL PHILOSOPHER

the ripe old age of 10 years old—you could expect to live another 32.2 years. In other words, you could be around until your early 40s, which certainly sounds more reasonable. And if you were truly blessed and happened to reach 25 years old without, say, catching the bubonic plague or being slaughtered by barbarians, you could expect to live until you were almost 50.

THAT STILL DOESN'T SOUND TOO GREAT.

No it doesn't, at least not when compared to our current expectations. But once again, we need some context. Just like today, we have to factor life circumstances into the mix. Back then, those who were living to these "extremes" were often the more affluent members of a community—landowners, the clergy, the wealthy and privileged. As a group, these people were better fed, better housed, and better cared for when they got sick.

As you might expect, the more affluent and privileged you were, the longer your lifespan. (It's a phenomenon that still exists today, clearly.) But back to the study mentioned above. In it, the authors researched the age at death of 80 popes. Their papacies were divided into two time periods spanning 1200-1900 AD. The first group of popes, who lived during the years 1200-1599, ascended to the papacy at the median age of 60 years old; they then ruled for about 6.5 years before dying.

In the second time period, from 1600-1900, the starting age of the new pontiffs had increased significantly. In this 300-year stretch, the median age of the newly elected Popes was 65.5 years, and they would go on to live, on average, another 11 years or so before dying.

What's interesting to note is that even in the Middle Ages, the pampered popes were regularly hitting their mid-60s before dying, with some making it to their early 70s before death caught up to them.

WOW. I ALWAYS THOUGHT THAT HUMAN LIFE EXPECTANCY WAS SHORT BACK THEN.

The human lifespan *was* short, relatively speaking—unless you were born into privilege. (Artists lived almost as long as their papist patrons, but this was likely because they also benefited from a healthier, less dangerous lifestyle by leveraging their talents to serve the upper classes.)

> **It is vanity to desire a long life and to take no heed of a good life.**
>
> —THOMAS À KEMPIS, WRITER AND THEOLOGIAN

Here's the upshot: our bodies, it seems, were always designed to last a lot longer than our ancestors' average lifespans would indicate. External factors, of course, cut lives short. Infant mortality was off the charts. Disease and pestilence would prematurely kill many. Poor nutrition, war, famine, poverty, unscientific or nonexistent health care—all help explain why those who weren't part of the elite barely managed to make it to the end of their 40s, at least in the Middle Ages.

So, there was, and is, a huge gulf between the haves and have-nots. It's never a good time to be in the latter camp, clearly.

BUT TODAY WE'RE LIVING LONGER. AREN'T WE?

We are.

WHEN DID THIS HAPPEN?

Life expectancy really started to ramp up around the start of the 1900s. In fact, over the past 120 years, we've seen our life expectancy increase by 30 years! Even in the U.S., which has lagged other western nations, there were about two full years added to life expectancy from 2000 to 2016. That's pretty recent, and pretty rapid.

Again, I'm not an expert. But even a layperson can quickly summarize many of the reasons for this. From improving general hygiene practices—disease and infection killed more soldiers than bullets in the U.S. Civil War—to the development of vaccines and the eradication of deadly diseases like smallpox, the last century has seen many advances in many areas.

Our progress has been astonishing. And still, it is at least somewhat beside the point.

WHY IS THIS "BESIDE THE POINT"?

As I've said a couple of times, it's one thing to extend the number of years you're here on earth. Not to diminish this, of course: we certainly have come a long way from the life expectancy of the Roman Empire. However, it's one thing to live a long life. It's quite another to live a long and *healthy* life.

So effectively, we're asking the wrong question. To paraphrase JFK, we should ask not how we can add years to our lives, but how we can add life to our years.

CAN YOU ELABORATE?

Of course. It's practically a buzzword now: we're talking about *healthspan*, or the number of years you are alive without having to endure significant health-related difficulties. This is a much more important metric than simply the amount of time you're here, taking up space—which is, unfortunately, what many of us end up doing. Warehoused in seniors' facilities, being fed through a tube, bedridden or disabled by obesity and chronic pain, never quite grasping where or even who you are because dementia has stolen your sense of self. Is this the way you want to check out?

WELL, NO—CLEARLY NOT.

Exactly. Think of the two concepts, lifespan and healthspan, as separate points on the same linear plane. For some of us living today, our lifespan will stretch to 100 and beyond. That's impressive, and it's much more than what we could have expected even a century ago. Now let's visualize healthspan, or the number of years during which we can expect at least a decent level of well-being.

Define it however you like. Maybe it's being able to drive your own car. Perhaps it has to do with physical mobility, or your ability to make your way through a tough crossword. Maybe it's important to you to be able to climb stairs or walk to the corner store to pick up a few vegetables and a carton of milk. Maybe seeing friends or family on a regular basis is what brings you joy. Perhaps you want it all.

Basically, it boils down to how long you can remain independent, capable, engaged,

> **Best estimates indicate that the average American can expect to celebrate only a single birthday in good health after the traditional retirement age of 65.**
>
> — DAVE A. CHOKSHI, PHYSICIAN AND FORMER NEW YORK CITY HEALTH COMMISSIONER, IN *THE NEW YORK TIMES*

and involved without being burdened by disease, disability, and decline. If you envision your problem-free years as a point on the same line as your lifespan, it will most often be placed earlier—unless, of course, you are struck down prematurely, which is obviously something that we don't want and often can't control.

The main point I'm making is that there is often a gulf between your healthy, problem-free years and the final years of your life. Do you want an example? According to the American Heart Association, the post-pandemic lifespan in the U.S. is 76 years. The average healthspan is 66 years. This means that for the average American, there's a 10-year gap between being alive and being alive healthily. We must shrink the space between those two points and do everything in our power to ensure that while we're living a long life, we are also stretching out our healthy years as long as possible.

SO HAS ANYONE EVER MEASURED HEALTHSPAN? ARE WE LIVING LONGER AND BETTER?

The best source I discovered was the World Health Organization, or WHO. They broke their data into a country-by-country table, as well as a region-by-region one, and came up with what they called a "healthy life expectancy at birth estimate," or HALE. According to WHO, this measures the "average number of years that a person can expect to live in 'full health' by taking into account years lived in less than full health due to disease and/or injury."

Quite a mouthful. In any event, there were some interesting results.

For one, all western nations are not created equal, or at least they're not delivering the same HALE numbers. We've already seen the major gap between lifespan and healthspan in the U.S. A 2023 opinion piece published in *The New York Times* summed up the American experience in the most depressing way possible: "Best estimates indicate that the average American can expect to celebrate only a single birthday in good health after the traditional retirement age of 65." Better book that cruise while you can.

However, some perspective is necessary. This is an average, just like 25 years was an average life expectancy for those born into the Roman Empire. The U.S. stats may reflect the more economically stratified nature of their society, as well as challenges that go hand in hand with their privately focused healthcare system. The upshot is still alarming: on average, Americans will spend 10 years of their lives in a state of less than "full" health.

> **When we say, 'Age is just a number,' what do we mean by this? In a nutshell, we're saying that you're only as old as you feel.**
>
> —JOHN BRINK

Oh, and the title of the *New York Times* article that raised this was, "Forget About Living to 100. Let's Live Healthier Instead." Talk about being on point!

HOW DO THOSE NUMBERS COMPARE TO OTHER NATIONS?

Favourably against some, less so against others. For example, they line up almost equally with Trinidad and Tobago or Serbia and are slightly ahead of Mexico. But other western industrialized nations are logging much better HALE numbers. Australia, New Zealand, Canada, Cyprus, Israel, Iceland, the entire European Union—all are posting HALE at birth numbers in the range of 70-plus years. Japan tops the list, at a little over 74 healthspan years.

So when we ask, "How long can we expect to live?" it's the wrong question. We should instead be asking, "How long can we expect to

> **It's cold comfort to live to 100 if you've been unable to remember who you are since the age of 84.**
>
> —JOHN BRINK

have *good health*? And more to the point, how can we extend our healthspan?" This is the question that should consume us. Simply by asking it, we change the way we think about how we live.

HOW CAN CHANGING THE QUESTION CHANGE OUR PERSPECTIVE?

You see, we are on what I call a *healthquest*. If framed this way, there are subtle but very real implications for how you look at your life. Living longer? Sure. Why not? But living better—*healthier*—is a much worthier goal. With this simple and seemingly small shift in focus, you open a door.

CAN YOU EXPLAIN THIS A BIT MORE?

Let me break it down. If the aim is to extend the amount of *time* people live, a certain mindset often follows. With some major exceptions—the campaign to stop people from smoking being a prime example—we tend to address health problems after they occur. We stress *intervention* over *prevention*. This is, for better and worse, the way our healthcare system is oriented.

Here's a common scenario. Every year, you see your GP. If you're lucky, they'll book off five minutes to see you. Generally, your visit will consist of some very general enquiries ("How have you been?" "Any concerns?"), maybe a quick check of your blood pressure. If you have a prescription for a chronic condition—anything from, say, high blood pressure to insomnia—you'll leave with the obligatory scrap of paper, which you'll present to your pharmacist to fill. You may also have to hit a lab to get your bloodwork done.

If there are no flags on your results, you'll wait for your next annual appointment—or, if you're unlucky, until some other underlying condition, unsuspected until now, lays you low. (Or worse.) Then the healthcare system kicks into high gear and does exactly what it's designed to do: intervene in something that requires immediate correction. Hopefully it ends well.

> **You know, some people say life is short and that you could get hit by a bus at any moment and that you have to live each day like it's your last. Bullshit. Life is long. You're probably not gonna get hit by a bus. And you're gonna have to live with the choices you make for the next fifty years.**
>
> —CHRIS ROCK, COMEDIAN

And here's the other thing: the healthcare system, as an intervention-oriented platform, is designed to treat whatever ails you. If it accomplishes this, success! Except for one not-so-minor detail.

WHICH IS?

The quality of life you're left with might not be so wonderful. Let's say, for example, that you're one of the millions of men over a certain age who regularly undergoes a prostate-specific antigen test, commonly known as a PSA test. It's highly effective and sensitive as hell. If your numbers exceed the threshold, and especially if your PSA score has changed dramatically from the last time it was measured, you may find yourself facing the prospect of invasive surgery for the removal of your *potentially* problematic prostate.

Prostate cancer can be a terrible and deadly disease, if it happens to be an aggressive strain. But many prostate tumours are not aggressive, and the process of prostate removal is fraught. As with any surgical procedure, things can and do go wrong. Post-surgery, you could have erectile difficulties where there were none before. Incontinence is also a possibility.

And if the tumour was either benign or extremely slow-growing—which many prostate tumours are—then the cure can sometimes be worse than the disease. Yet by intervening surgically, *the healthcare system did its job*. It stepped in to remove a threat.

So if the question is "How can I ensure that I increase my lifespan?" then surgery is a good option. However, if what you actually want is to extend your *healthspan*, to increase the time where your body doesn't get in the way of you enjoying your life, then in some cases it's not nearly so cut and dried.

OKAY, I GET IT.

And there's another question we should be looking at, too. How old are you?

I'M NOT SURE WHERE YOU'RE HEADING WITH THIS. IS IT A TRICK QUESTION?

In a way, I suppose it is. But not really. When we say, "Age is just a number," what do we mean by this? In a nutshell, we're saying, "You're only as old as you feel." Your chronological age is only one marker of how "old" you are, and in my opinion, it's not the most important one. What matters a whole lot more is your *biological* age: where your current state of health situates you on a timeline relative to others.

According to your health at this moment, how old are you? To me, this is what biological age implies. The first thing we must do is try to nail this down as best we can.

HOW CAN BIOLOGICAL AGE BE DETERMINED?

Good question! I admit I went down a rabbit hole when I first started looking into this. At the most basic level, there are online questionnaires that can give you a ballpark idea of whether your current health and basic lifestyle conform to your chronological age or if they imply a different biological or "real" age. But their accuracy is sometimes debatable.

Many of these tests try to determine lifestyle and health variables—everything from how much alcohol you drink and how many leafy green vegetables you regularly eat to your exercise, stress, and activity levels. Do you have a group of close friends? How many? How much water do you drink? How long do you usually go between meals?

All of this is designed to try to capture a portrait of the way you live. But like a poorly executed police criminal sketch, the portrait that emerges can bear little resemblance to the person it's supposedly capturing.

IT'S PRETTY MUCH A WASH, THEN?

No, not necessarily. The online questionnaires have their place, even if it's only to start you thinking about certain lifestyle choices that may not be in your best interests. But often, as with any self-reporting, there is ample room for self-delusion. In my experience, people can lie the most easily when it comes to looking at themselves.

ARE THERE ANY OBJECTIVE TESTS THAT CAN HELP US KNOW OUR BIOLOGICAL AGE?

There are, although I'm not in a position to judge or recommend them. In 2013, Steve Horvath, a UCLA research scientist, developed what is reportedly the first reliable epigenetic, or biological, age clock. In a nutshell, according to a 2023 online *Fortune* article, he discovered that "multiple tissue types could be used to calculate a person's biological age." Now, he's marketing myDNAge, a testing kit that uses this age clock as a basis to determine biological age.

Please don't ask me to explain the process, which involves "methylation of DNA"!

AND THIS TEST IS FREELY AVAILABLE?

Well, "freely" is not the word I'd use: it costs USD $299. And it will take about six weeks for your results to be emailed to you after you submit a blood sample. But let's circle back to why we'd consider doing this in the first place. If we can establish our biological age independent of our chronological age, it will give us an indication of how much "headroom" we have, in terms of our lifespan—and hopefully our healthspan, too.

For example, if your chronological age is 60 but your test indicates that your health is more in line with the average 75-year-old's, then your predicted healthspan is much less than you'd probably expect. But even though this is a negative, knowing this number can inspire you to make the kind of healthy choices that could narrow the gap between your chronological age and your biological age—like exercising more or eating better. Your estimated healthspan not a fixed number, by the way. Lifestyle changes can actually impact it.

Or maybe your biological age is *lower* than your chronological age. Maybe you're 62 and have the biological markers of a 58-year-old. That's great! It also presents you with certain choices you'll need to make. For example, if your body could last until you reach, say, the chronological age of 100, you'd better make sure that you're prepared for that eventuality. Financially, you'll need to be able to sustain a decent standard of living. Your social circles will need to be strong, since many people who outlive family and friends struggle to find meaning. Remember that for a lot of us, the potential for serious cognitive decline can also be a factor. It's cold comfort to live to 100 if you've been unable to remember who you are since the age of 84.

> **You can live to be a hundred if you give up all the things that make you want to live to be a hundred.**
>
> —WOODY ALLEN, WRITER, ACTOR, AND DIRECTOR

Again, though, it's all about establishing a baseline, or snapshot, of your current state of health. That will allow you to make smart choices to ensure, as best you can, that you live a long time and remain well.

HAVE YOU DONE THIS KIND OF TESTING?

As of this writing, I haven't. We'll see.

ARE THERE ANY OTHER WAYS TO ASSESS YOUR CURRENT STATE OF HEALTH?

Absolutely. Although I've come a bit late to the party, wearable technology—most commonly the smartwatch—is a giant leap forward. I say this for at least three reasons.

First, we can now monitor, in real time, an incredible amount of data in a way that's simple, easy, and not at all invasive. Even an entry-level smartwatch will track your resting heart rate, how often you move, how many steps you take, and how many stairs you climb. If you wear it while you sleep—and you should—it will track additional variables like your sleep patterns, resting heart rate, breathing rate, and heart rate variability, or HRV.

Second, it allows researchers to tap into health data that is now being collected on a massive scale. True, these are not controlled trials with strictly defined parameters, but they reveal an enormous amount of information about the overall health of those who participate. The bottom line? Almost everyone who wears a fitness tracker gives up a lot of data. For once, this is probably a net positive, although the potential for misuse is definitely there.

Third—and this relates to the first point—many smartwatches are designed to flag certain health conditions, such as an irregular heartbeat.

THAT'S GOT TO BE A RARE THING, ISN'T IT?

Again, I'm not a doctor, so I'd be remiss in giving out medical advice. In any case, there are quite a few important issues beyond overnight heart irregularity that these smartwatches flag. Here's an anecdotal situation that I know of. A friend of mine has always snored. When I say "snored," I mean house-shaking, jackhammer-on-concrete levels of noise. I'm not sure how his partner can sleep, to be honest. It would be like lying next to a leaf blower all night.

At one point, my friend mentioned his snoring to his doctor, who in turn asked whether he was sleepy during the day, or whether anyone has ever noticed him not breathing at night—some of the standard questions designed to determine if he might have obstructive sleep apnea. But aside from age and snoring, my friend had no indicators that would point to a diagnosis, and he exhibited no symptoms, none at all. A lot of people snore, he reminded himself. It probably wasn't an issue.

Then my friend started wearing a smartwatch to bed. Within a few weeks, he began to notice a pattern. One of the things that his watch tracked was changes in his blood-oxygen saturation, or SpO2, while he slept. Some nights it was fine, with very little variation, but on other nights, his blood-oxygen levels would vary a lot. Sometimes the variations were extreme and happened for much of the night.

He went back to his doctor and showed him the results from a few nights of tracking. The doctor immediately referred him for an overnight sleep-apnea assessment, which you can now do in the comfort of your home.

WHAT WERE THE RESULTS?

The respiratory therapist assigned to him told him he did indeed have sleep apnea—moderate bordering on severe. He was having some sort of apnea event 28 times an hour, meaning his body and brain were going without oxygen for at least 10 seconds every two minutes all night. Now he's getting used to a "continuous positive airway pressure machine," or CPAP, which blows air into his nostrils all night. His nightly oxygen variation is consistently low, and the number of apnea-related events he experiences at night are close to normal levels.

Sleep apnea is a significant health condition. It is associated with diabetes risk, elevated blood pressure, heart disease, and stroke. If he had never strapped on a smartwatch, who knows where his health might have headed?

DO YOU HAVE A SMARTWATCH?

Absolutely. For a while now I've been wearing it 24 hours a day. That way, it tracks a lot of metrics that you wouldn't normally be able to access.

For example, here's a snapshot from a normal week. My resting heart rate averaged 62 beats per minute, or BPM. Considering that trained athletes of a much younger vintage often register in the 40 to 60 BPM range, I'm feeling pretty good about that.

WHAT EXACTLY DOES THE RESTING HEART RATE MEASURE?

It basically measures your heart rate when you're not exerting yourself—when you're sitting during the day, or when you're sleeping. It matters because it's an indicator of overall fitness, and the lower the number, generally speaking, the better. Most people fall into the 60 to 100 BPM range. For my age, where I'm at is a very good result.

WHAT OTHER METRICS ARE YOU TRACKING?

Let's see. The standard things like the number of steps I take in a day and the number of floors I climb. Those are givens and, obviously, they can vary a lot from day to day. But others, like heart rate variability, or HRV, are also part of the data set. HRV is also a key indicator of overall health. It's collected while you sleep and tracks the variation in the number of milliseconds between heart beats. In this case, higher is better, because it signals your body's ability to toggle between fight-or-flight mode and rest-and-digest mode. Mine averaged 23 over a week recently.

IS THAT GOOD?

Not if I were 14 years old. If I were, I'd be in trouble, since the average values for a teenager are almost 80. But I'm almost 84, and HRV goes down exponentially with age. Factoring this in, I'm right in the pocket for men aged 77 and over.

But the most important smartwatch metric probably isn't HRV, or even BPM. It's V02 max, which measures how efficiently your body uses oxygen when it's under peak cardio stress—in other words, when you're really working it. As with HRV, the higher the number, the better. Some have described it as the "gold standard" of fitness indicators. And again, context is necessary to fully understand the results. Age matters, and your score can increase or decrease as your fitness level goes up or down. My V02 max score is 35.2.

IS THAT A GOOD OUTCOME?

Again, it depends. If I were between 30 and 39 years old, it would be classified as "poor." If I were between 50-59 years old, it would be "good." But for a man of my age, a V02 max score of 35.2 is classed as "superior." I'll take it. I was happy with the results, no question about it. But even if it had come up short—if, for example, my smartwatch data had indicated a potential problem—I would rather know about it and deal with it sooner rather than later.

Or, worse-case scenario, before it was way too late. Because, first, I want to extend the quality of my life—to ensure that I live *well*, not just *long*. And second, I'm at the point in my own timeline where people often come down with what they call "diseases of ageing." We'll take a look at those in the next chapter.

CHAPTER THREE

TIME WAITS FOR NO ONE? NAVIGATING AGE-RELATED ILLNESS

Some say that the process of dying begins immediately after we're born. While it's a sobering thought, it's probably more hyperbole than fact. However, something significant does happen to our bodies as we age—and often, it's not particularly pleasant. Dementia. Heart attack, stroke, and other cardiovascular diseases. Cancers, terrifying and often relentless in their assaults. Simple things like slipping on the ice outside, potentially starting an irreversible decline. So why are our bodies, despite being so well designed, prone to problems that can severely affect quality of life?

YOU MENTION THAT OUR BODIES ARE "WELL DESIGNED." WHAT EXACTLY DO YOU MEAN BY THIS?

I'm really just stating the obvious: considering the amount of wear and tear that all of us put on our bodies, it's incredible that we make it past our teenaged years. I'm reminded of the first time I saw Michelangelo's statue of David: the muscular arms, the rippled pectorals and, of course, the hands—they always get talked about. As a competitive bodybuilder, I can't describe the kind of awe that this inspires. By so expertly crafting this idealized picture of strength and health, Michelangelo created a celebration of human possibility.

But as it stands, even though we're well designed, there are limits to how long we can last. And again, it's not necessarily the length of time before our bodies give out, but how long our bodies function in an unimpeded way. At risk of hitting you over the head with this, we want to extend our *healthspans*, not just our lifespans.

Obviously, I'd like to do both. As you know, I'm planning to live to 120—best-laid plans of mice and men excepted, of course. But honestly, I'd be happy to go out like Olga Kotelko did.

I'M SORRY, WHO IS OLGA KOTELKO?

I mentioned her briefly in the introduction. Olga was a storied Canadian track-and-field athlete. Over the course of her life, she collected more than 30 world records and 750-plus gold medals in the Masters category, completely dominating her age group. And here's the kicker: she was 77 years old when she took up competitive track and field. According to Bruce Grierson, who first wrote about her in *The New York Times Magazine*, "She is considered one of the world's greatest athletes." Quite something, really. Born in Saskatchewan, Ukrainian heritage, no real interest in or aptitude for sports—and then...

Bruce was captivated by Olga's story and spent five years fleshing it out in his book, *What Makes Olga Run? The Mystery of the 90-Something Track Star and What She Can Teach Us About Living Longer, Happier Lives*. But Olga was more than an athlete. During the writing of the book, she was also basically a lab rat, someone who over several years was the subject of scientific and medical tests. Bruce was along for the ride, documenting the whole thing.

AND WHAT DID THEY FIND? DID OLGA HAVE SOME SUPER-HEROIC GENES OR SOMETHING?

Actually, no. Interestingly, when she was younger, she smoked cigarettes. And she'd have a drink or two, though only occasionally. She ate very little processed food, however.

WAS THERE ANYTHING OLGA WAS DOING ON A REGULAR BASIS THAT MAY HAVE ACCOUNTED FOR HER HEALTH?

Well, she did eat a lot of fish—pickled herring, for example, which offers additional benefits because of the fermentation process that's used to prepare it. But really, Olga's habits, and how she lived, weren't designed as an intentional process. She simply was who she was and ate what she was familiar with. Some of the underlying causes of her amazing health were just luck.

"By accident, with her diet and her exercise routines, she did everything right," says Grierson. "Even growing up on a farm, that's not something she chose, but it maps onto a healthy, long life just because of the activity, the diet you end up eating out there, the air you breathe." Plus, he notes, farms can be mini "Blue Zones" because the people who live there do lots of outdoor activity and very little sitting around.

BUT WERE THERE ANY BIOLOGICAL MARKERS THAT COULD HAVE BEEN RESPONSIBLE?

Possibly, but even with the number of tests that Olga went through on her journey, a lot of it ends up being at least a bit speculative. "Perhaps part of what's protecting her is her own mind," writes Grierson. "That is, she is refusing to become a wizened little old lady at the normal rate because she simply does not believe she is one."

I agree: in my opinion, part of what can keep us healthy and feeling young is our attitude. If that piece of the puzzle is in place, you just might be able, as Bruce says, to "run between the raindrops." In other words, you might dodge the fate that awaits many of us as we age.

To look at it from another perspective, Olga was what they call a "super senior."

WHAT'S A "SUPER SENIOR"?

The original Super Seniors were a group of study subjects, aged 85 to 105, who were free of the usual diseases of ageing, such as cancer, diabetes, heart disease, and dementia. Now the term is used for a person who's over 85 and who has managed to avoid having a chronic condition or major life-ending disease. This puts them in the top 1% for healthspan. Compare that to the average American 75-year-old, who, according to the latest statistics, has three major chronic conditions and is on at least four prescription medications.

> **For building cognition, Sudoku is a shovel, and exercise is a bulldozer.**
>
> —BRUCE GRIERSON, AUTHOR, IN *WHAT MAKES OLGA RUN?*

The good news? Once you make it this far, your odds of never succumbing to diseases such as cancer, diabetes, heart failure, and Alzheimer's actually get better.

WHY IS THIS?

Well, speaking figuratively, you dodged the proverbial bullet. Of course, this doesn't guarantee that you'll live to 100, or, as seems more and more possible, 120. There are other *gotchas!* lurking. In fact, there are more than a few, even outside of the major afflictions.

Olga finally succumbed to one *gotcha!*, and she couldn't have seen it coming. A few months before she passed, Olga admitted to Bruce that she felt a little flat, but when she died—at home, puttering in her garden, of a brain bleed—it was only days after she'd participated in a track meet, where she broke yet another couple of records.

The point is, there was no gap between Olga's healthspan and her lifespan. There was no lingering illness, no cognitive decline, no lengthy hospital stay, no being fed through a tube. She avoided all the chronic conditions and major afflictions that strike down so many of us before our time. She was here, at age 95, vibrant and robust, and then suddenly she wasn't.

WHAT ARE THE "CHRONIC CONDITIONS AND MAJOR AFFLICTIONS," AS YOU PUT IT?

We'll get into this shortly. First, I'd like to take some time to talk about what "ageing" is.

WELL, IT'S OBVIOUS, ISN'T IT? IT MEANS "GETTING OLDER."

It does, of course. Scientifically speaking, though, it means more than that. It implies processes that typically go hand in hand with *senescence*. Senescence is about your cells—specifically, a state where they age and stop dividing but don't die.

Again, I have to caution you that I'm not an expert. But there is a solid body of evidence pointing to certain processes that are associated with this kind of decline. I promise I won't get too technical, but we do need to dip our toe into something called "oxidative stress."

SO WHAT IS "OXIDATIVE STRESS"? AND HOW DOES IT AFFECT US?

I'll have to crib my answer from Wikipedia, because there's clearly a limit to my understanding:

> *Oxidative stress reflects an imbalance between the systemic manifestation of reactive oxygen species and a biological system's ability to readily detoxify the reactive intermediates or to repair the resulting damage. Disturbances in the normal redox state of cells can cause toxic effects through the production of peroxides and free radicals that damage all components of the cell, including proteins, lipids, and DNA.*

Basically, it's a process where we can increasingly no longer cleanse or repair the damage to our own cells. And this process, some have concluded, is what causes us to age.

THAT ALL SEEMS KIND OF MIND-BOGGLING.

Agreed! Just to emphasize again, though: this is an oversimplification of some very complex biological interactions and how they affect us physiologically.

And herein lies the danger: no matter how much we read, no matter how reputable the sources we access, there is so much room to misunderstand—or, worse, fall prey to many of the charlatans who operate in this space. A good rule of thumb is, if "medical knowledge" comes along with a sales pitch—you know, "Buy Our Supplements to Reverse Oxidative Stress and Beat Ageing!"—you have my permission to run as far and as fast as you can.

Instead of me trying to explain what I barely comprehend, let's pull back a bit and look at the bigger picture, which is that internal processes are responsible for both ageing and the kind of conditions that often go hand in hand with it. Oxidative stress is implicated in many of the kind of diseases and conditions that tend to plague us as we age.

WHAT ARE THE MOST COMMON CONDITIONS?

In *Outlive: The Science and Art of Longevity*, Canadian-born Dr. Peter Attia calls the most prominent threats the "Four Horsemen." These are chronic conditions that, statistically, will end up killing most of us living today: heart disease, cancer, Alzheimer's (and related neurodegenerative diseases), and type 2 diabetes (and related metabolic dysfunction).

We'll talk about them all a little later, and they'll pop up throughout the book. I should mention here and now that although I like what Attia has to say, as a writer I have my own views about the way he says it.

WHAT DO YOU MEAN?

He's a doctor, so he's obviously far more conversant—and comfortable—with medical jargon and terminology than I am. But I'm also ADHD, and his book was a hard slog, to be honest. That's the exact opposite of what I hope I'm doing here. All this said, it's really beside the point. What Attia really brings to the table is an attitude: that if you identify potential danger signs early on and make the kind of choices you need to make, there is every possibility that, first, you'll extend your healthy years, and second, you'll be more likely to avoid the chronic conditions we've just mentioned.

As we briefly discussed in the last chapter, we need to know who we are before we can address what should be done. And that's another bonus point for Attia: he's a great believer in medical testing as one of the building blocks of a personalized, targeted healthcare plan.

CAN YOU GIVE US AN EXAMPLE?

Sure. Check out *Limitless*, a National Geographic television series that explores longevity and how to live your life to be the healthiest you can be for as long as you can. The series follows the actor Chris Hemsworth, best known for playing Thor in the Marvel film series of the same name. By any measure, Hemsworth is a very fit individual: strapping and muscled, 6'3" tall, the kind of guy whose physical presence basically defines good health—outwardly, at least.

I'M GUESSING THERE'S A "BUT" LURKING IN HERE...

You're right. In one of the *Limitless* episodes, Dr. Attia puts Hemsworth through a battery of tests, which are a key part of Attia's standard treatment plan. While most of Hemsworth's results were excellent, there was one marker that caused concern.

WHICH WAS...?

One of the genetic tests revealed the presence of apolipoprotein E4, otherwise known as ApoE4, a gene variant that has been linked with a greater chance of developing Alzheimer's disease. It's not uncommon—around 25% of people have it—but it is significant. Carrying one copy in your DNA doubles or triples your chances of developing Alzheimer's, compared to those who don't carry the gene.

But Hemsworth fell into a different, much smaller category. He had not one, but *two copies* of the ApoE4 variant. This puts him in a subset that includes only 2% to 3% of the population, those who've inherited it from both the maternal and paternal sides. This raises the risk of getting Alzheimer's disease substantially—about 8 to 10 times over someone without the gene. Plus, it's also correlated with earlier onset of Alzheimer's symptoms. Hemsworth, whose grandfather currently struggles with Alzheimer's, was visibly shaken by the reveal.

A STAGED REACTION, PROBABLY. I MEAN, THE GUY'S AN ACTOR, RIGHT?

It was not acting. Hemsworth was *devastated*. So much so that as of now, he's on hiatus from acting and is instead concentrating on his health and his family. Does that sound like someone who's trying to pull a fast one to raise the drama stakes? I don't think so. But even though this was a soul-crushing revelation, it doesn't necessarily mean that Hemsworth will be stricken with Alzheimer's. It's just a loud, ringing alarm bell, one that he clearly heard and is doing his level best to address.

HOW CAN HE "ADDRESS" IT? IT'S SOMETHING THAT HAPPENS ON A GENETIC LEVEL, RIGHT? IF THAT'S THE CASE, THERE'S NOT MUCH YOU CAN DO, I'D THINK.

Ah, but you'd think wrong! Even though the risk is inherited, Dr. Attia says there are lifestyle changes that Hemsworth can make that could help. One is eating well, with an emphasis on getting enough omega-3 fatty acids, which are often found in fatty fish such as salmon.

Exercise is vitally important, as is getting enough sleep. There's also a case to be made for learning: when it comes to Alzheimer's, higher education seems to be preventative. Apparently if you build up your "cognitive reserves," you'll be less likely to have an issue with dementia.

The bottom line is, your fate may not be completely out of your hands. That's reassuring.

BEFORE YOU SAID THAT THERE MIGHT BE HOPE FOR HIM, I WAS ABOUT TO SAY THAT IT MIGHT HAVE BEEN BETTER IF HEMSWORTH NEVER UNDERGONE THE TESTING.

Sure—except for the possibility that by making lifestyle changes today, he might be able to stave off Alzheimer's later in life. Many doctors would agree with your sentiment, though, and would hesitate to advise their patients to get this testing done. It's a fairly widespread perspective and yes, there are definitely downsides to knowing this kind of thing. I'd advise anyone thinking of going down this road to discuss the options with a genetic counsellor. In Canada, the Canadian Association of Genetic Counsellors would be a good place to start.

All this said, if there is even a slim chance that you can alter the course of what seems to be your "fate," then I'd suggest doing it.

OKAY, BUT IS THIS KIND OF TESTING EVEN COVERED BY HEALTH INSURANCE?

I can't answer that, since coverage varies so much depending on where you are and what kind of coverage you have. That's a conundrum that seems to be baked into this: is "knowing thyself" something that's just for the wealthy?

Peter Attia has been asked this before, in an interview with *The New York Times*. His take is that, beyond the expense, the real investment you have to make is in time. All of this takes time, and that's the resource that so many of us lack.

SO LET'S SAY I DODGE CANCER, HEART DISEASE, AND DIABETES, THE OTHER THREE OF THE "FOUR HORSEMEN." STATISTICALLY, AM I IN THE CLEAR?

Well, to inject a little real-world perspective into this, you could get hit by the proverbial bus tomorrow. More seriously, there are other afflictions that can accompany ageing. A big one is something that many of us simply take for granted: frailty.

BUT THAT'S JUST A GIVEN, RIGHT? AS YOU GET OLDER, YOU GET FRAILER.

You're only partly correct. We do lose physical ability with age, which is why it's so important to incorporate strength training into exercise routines before you lose too much muscle mass. But even though we think we know what we're talking about, I think it might be best if we define "frailty" and get on the same page.

Again, I'm not an expert, which is something I'll be saying a lot as we go on this journey together. Here's a comprehensive definition from the journal *Free Radical Biology and Medicine*:

> *Frailty could be defined as the biological syndrome of a decreased reserve and resistance to stressors, resulting from cumulative declines throughout multiple physiologic systems, and causing vulnerability to adverse outcomes.*

In "the field," if I can put it that way, there are five main signs of frailty: being weak, walking slowly, having a low activity level, losing weight without meaning to, and reporting feelings of exhaustion. According to the article, if you have three or more of these, you have frailty.

That's a little more tightly nailed down, I think.

YES, THAT'S MORE EXACT THAN WHAT I WAS THINKING.

Frankly, me too. And it turns out, frailty is more than a minor problem: it's a serious condition that sets the stage for other health difficulties. Take falls, for example. Did you know that, according to the WHO, about a third of people aged 70 and older worldwide experience falls? In Canada, falls are the number-one injury-related cause of hospitalizations and death and the sixth-most-common cause of death in people 85 years and older.

LEADING CAUSES OF DEATH IN CANADA, 2019.

	RANK	NUMBER	%
Total, all causes of death		**284,082**	**100.0**
Cancer	1	80,152	28.2
Diseases of the heart	2	52,541	18.5
Accidents (unintentional injuries)	3	13,746	4.8
Cerebrovascular diseases	4	13,660	4.8
Chronic lower respiratory diseases	5	12,823	4.5
Diabetes mellitus	6	6,912	2.4
Influenza and pneumonia	7	6,893	2.4
Alzheimer's disease	8	6,166	2.2
Suicide	9	4,012	1.4
Kidney diseases (nephritis, nephrotic syndrome and nephrosis)	10	3,767	1.2
All other causes of death	-	83,410	29.4

Source: Statistics Canada, 2020.

About a third of all people admitted to hospital for falling have broken their hip—something that can lead to rapidly declining overall health. In fact, 21% of people who have their hip fracture surgically repaired die within a year, and a staggering 70% of those whose fracture is not repaired will die before the year is out!

Falls are epidemic, and outcomes are serious. And there's a vicious cycle that often sets in. Once the person "recovers," they are probably less strong than before they fell. Being less strong, they tend to avoid exercise, or even going outside in winter, for fear they'll take another spill. Being less active leads them to a sedentary lifestyle, which increases their frailty and makes them more likely to fall.

And of course, the frequency and severity of injury from falls increases as you age.

HAVE YOU EVER EXPERIENCED A FALL?

I have, and fairly recently. I was leaving the office and slipped on the steps leading to the mill yard. I flew in the air and landed with a sickening thud. Then I got up, dusted myself off, and went about my day. I even worked out.

The moral is obvious: if you maintain your strength, events that could cripple someone else may have no effect on you. I fell. I got up. I went on with my day. But the thing is, I work out, regularly and rigorously. It's no accident—pun intended!—that I was unhurt.

CANCER, DIABETES, ALZHEIMER'S, HEART DISEASE AND STROKE, FRAILTY AND FALLING... IT KIND OF SOUNDS LIKE AGEING IS A MINEFIELD. I SHOULD JUST STAY AT HOME, CLOSE THE BLINDS, AND WEAR A SUIT MADE FROM BUBBLE WRAP.

I know you're kidding, but honestly, that's the worst thing you can do. Aside from the lack of fresh air and just being immobile, there's another age-related illness that people simply don't talk about.

And that's loneliness.

There are many poor health outcomes associated with being lonely and isolated (see sidebar, "Health Risks of Loneliness"). The fact that the CDC says that loneliness "significantly increases a person's risk of premature death from all causes" really hits home.

Still, the conditions you mention are the age-related outcomes that we want to avoid. Aside from age in general, there are other factors we have to look at to get the full picture of the risks we may face, and what we can do limit them.

HEALTH RISKS OF LONELINESS

Many people think loneliness and isolation are the same thing, but they're actually distinct states. Loneliness means a negative feeling of being alone or separated from others. (Depending on your personality, you could feel fine when you're alone—or, conversely, lonely even when you're around other people.) Isolation is about social connection. It is defined as having few social contacts or people to interact with.

Although it's hard to measure social isolation and loneliness precisely, there is strong evidence that many adults aged 50 and older are socially isolated or lonely in ways that put their health at risk. Studies have found the following:

- Isolation increases a person's risk of premature death from all causes by a level equivalent to smoking 15 cigarettes a day and is associated with a 50% higher risk of dementia.
- Poor social relationships are associated with a 29% increased risk of heart disease and a 32% increased risk of stroke.
- Loneliness is associated with higher rates of depression, anxiety, and suicide, as well as obesity, smoking, and alcohol abuse.
- Loneliness among heart-failure patients is associated with a quadrupled risk of death, 68% higher risk of hospitalization, and 57% higher risk of emergency-department visits.

Sources: U.S. Centers for Disease Control; National Institute on Aging, "Loneliness and Social Isolation—Tips for Staying Connected"; Cigna Healthcare.

SECTION TWO

GENETICS, ENVIRONMENT, AND LIFESTYLE

"God, grant me the serenity to accept the things I cannot change, the courage to change the things I can, and the wisdom to know the difference."

—Serenity Prayer

CHAPTER FOUR

BLUE GENES? THE IMPACT OF GENETICS

Some people are born lucky—others, not so much. When it comes to health, many believe that much hinges on your genetic makeup. But is this true? How much do your genes factor into your healthspan? Is there any way to change this? Is your biological clock set at birth? What about trauma? Does ethnicity play a role? Can life events alter your genetic makeup? Once you know your "genetic score," can you do anything to change it? If so, what?

SO HOW DO GENETICS FACTOR INTO THE HEALTH MATRIX?

First, a story. When I was younger, every day on the way to and from school I would pass by a seniors' care facility in my village. Back then, we'd call them "old folks' homes," which of course doesn't land well on the ear today. They were basically warehouses, and the product they stocked was the aged and the infirm. I'd see them being pushed around in wheelchairs by nursing staff who often looked uninterested in being there.

I carry this picture around in my head like a photo in a wallet. Something about it was simply terrifying to me. Part of my fear was probably inherited.

HOW SO?

My father was also disturbed by that seniors' facility. Maybe it triggered something deep within, a fear that he would someday be a resident there too. "Jann," he would say, "I really don't want to end up here." He wasn't necessarily talking about this specific place—more, I think, about being in a situation where he would need this kind of care. My dad's father had died suddenly and at a young age. I think when that sort of thing happens, the trauma can instil a fear that death is stalking you, even when you're outwardly healthy.

So the care facility was, I believe, a reminder to my father of his impending mortality. The sad irony is that that he *did* end up there, in that very facility. All things considered, it was by far the best place to take care of his needs.

This sort of story is repeated again and again. When my friend Robert was younger, he had a very close relationship with his maternal grandmother, Eliza. But as he got a little older, a stiffness settled over Eliza's interactions with Robert, and a relationship that was once warm and loving became strained and awkward. It was like a meeting between strangers.

When Eliza finally died, at the age of 101, she had spent several years in a care facility in a state of dementia and didn't recognize her own children. She had lived a long life, but it wasn't a very good life for her final years.

THAT'S A SAD STORY—BUT, LIKE YOU SAY, IT'S A VERY COMMON ONE.

It is. And here's where it intersects the topic at hand. Eliza's daughter—Robert's mom—was horrified by the transformation her own mother had undergone and what it had done to their relationships. "If I ever start acting like that, you have to tell me," she said to Robert on more than one occasion.

Within the decade, sadly, Robert did have to tell her—or rather, try to tell her. But his mother had already pulled away from her children in much the same way that Eliza had, and now she was unwilling or unable to be the person she'd been throughout Robert's life. A rift developed in the family, with Robert and his youngest sister becoming basically estranged from their mother.

Robert knows now that his mother's fear was less about becoming distant from her children than about the underlying cause of that distance—namely, dementia. Her fear was well-founded. By the time she died, at 85, she did have dementia, probably in an advanced stage. By withdrawing from two of her three children and aligning with their remaining adult sibling, who had always lived in the family home, she blew the family apart. Really, though, she had few options regarding how things eventually played out. She was almost certainly up against a genetic predisposition to dementia.

HOW MUCH OF A FACTOR DO GENES PLAY IN LIFE EXPECTANCY?

Well, to bring the conversation back to the topic at hand, let's note that neither woman's predisposition to dementia seems to have shortened her life: one lived to over 100, the other to 85. What it did shorten was their *healthspan*. When they were lucid, neither would have chosen to end their days as they did or wanted to cause their children psychological harm. But this is what happened.

> **Scientists speculate that for the first seven or eight decades, lifestyle is a stronger determinant of health and life span than genetics. Eating well, not drinking too much alcohol, avoiding tobacco, and staying physically active enable some individuals to attain a healthy old age; genetics then appears to play a progressively important role in keeping individuals healthy as they age into their eighties and beyond. Many nonagenarians and centenarians are able to live independently and avoid age-related diseases until the very last years of their lives.**
>
> —U.S. NATIONAL LIBRARY OF MEDICINE

To get back to your question, though, the main answer is that it's one that researchers are working hard to answer. One of the most referenced studies on the impact of genetics is the so-called "Danish Twins Study" from 1996. It looked at 2,872 twins born in Denmark between 1870 and 1900 and tried to determine whether life expectancy was correlated with heredity. It was—but only to a modest degree. The authors determined that only 25% of longevity was heritable—in other words, a result of genetics. Presumably this means that the other 75% originates in environmental and lifestyle factors.

Remarkably, this 25%-75% split is still the figure that scientists are arriving at today, even after decades more research. And the exciting new field of epigenetics is starting to show why. Researchers are discovering that just having a gene—for, say, being more likely to get a certain kind of cancer, or, conversely, *less* likely to get a certain kind of cancer—isn't all there is to it. Many of those genes either get "switched on" or "switched off" in response to our lifestyle habits, life events, and environment.

The main culprits for "turning on" harmful genes? You won't be surprised to learn that so far, they seem to be the usual suspects: smoking, drinking, eating poorly, sleeping poorly, and not exercising enough. And the factors in turning on helpful genes, or keeping harmful ones turned off, are the opposite: eating well, refraining from smoking and drinking, getting enough sleep, and exercising.

The best proof of how epigenetics influence us is, again, twin studies—specifically, studies of identical twins, who start out life with exactly the same genes. More than one-third of twins in epigenetic studies have significantly different genes than their "identical" sibling—and the older they get, the more differences they are likely to have.

Ultimately, that's very good news.

WHY DO YOU SAY THAT?

Because it means that much of what affects our ability to live a long and healthy life falls outside of what some might call "fate." While it's impossible to choose what genes we get from our parents, it turns out that we have a lot of influence over what those genes do. Combine that influence over genetic factors with our significant ability to decide on lifestyle and environment factors, and it adds up to a huge amount of control over what happens to our health. So the fact that, say, a person's

> **Genes are not your destiny. You can win the tug of war against your genes.**
>
> —DR. RICHARD ISAACSON, WEILL CORNELL MEDICAL COLLEGE

father and grandfather died of cancer doesn't necessarily mean they are going to go the same way.

That said, there is an increased risk of acquiring some conditions that "run in the family." People who have a family history of certain types of cancer, type 2 diabetes, Alzheimer's, and cardiovascular disease, for example, need to be aware that genetics may play a more significant role in their health than most others.

DO YOU HAVE ANY EXAMPLES OF CASES WHERE A GENETIC PREDISPOSITION IS CLEARCUT?

Absolutely. A few years ago, a woman I know was at a crossroads. When she was young, her mother had died of breast cancer. Since then, two of her older siblings had also passed away from the same disease. She had a choice to make, but she needed it to be an informed decision. So she chose to go the genetic testing route.

Unfortunately, the tests revealed that she carried the genetic mutation that would predispose her to breast cancer. Now, as I understand it, that outcome would not have been a certainty. But the fear loomed large. She had a husband and children. She didn't want her life cut short. The statistical likelihood that she would end up travelling the same road as her mother and sisters was too frightening to leave to chance.

So she opted for the only measure that would guarantee that she could dodge this: a double mastectomy. She made the decision after having weighed all the possible outcomes. The procedure gave her much more than an excellent chance at a long life: it gave her peace of mind. Can you imagine living day to day knowing that inside you there was a ticking time bomb? How much stress would that put on someone? And how might that stress eventually be expressed? As we now know, stress can take a huge toll on the physical self. I firmly believe that health is holistic: mind, body, and spirit must be in alignment.

And so she made a well-considered choice to do whatever it took to remain healthy. To give the middle finger to fate, as it were.

IS THERE USUALLY A GENETIC ELEMENT TO CANCER?

Not at all. Lung cancer, for example, usually develops because of environmental and lifestyle factors—or, to be blunt about it, from one lifestyle factor: smoking. There is a reason, though, that when you see a family doctor for the first time or fill out a life-insurance form, you're asked about the health histories of your parents and siblings, and sometimes your grandparents, too.

OKAY, SAY YOU HAVE A GENETIC PREDISPOSITION TO SOMETHING—CANCER, ALZHEIMER'S, WHATEVER. WHAT CAN YOU DO TO REDUCE YOUR RISK?

I'm glad you phrased the question like that. Because you're exactly correct: it is about *reducing* risk, not about eliminating it. The one thing that keeps evolving is the way we treat these conditions. For example, a 2023 *New York Times* article reported on a new drug called *donanemab*, an interventionist therapy designed to slow the progression of Alzheimer's. In trials, it was modestly successful in doing this, at least in early-stage patients who had a certain protein that produces "tangles" in the brain.

The problem with these "breakthroughs" is that they seem to come along with great regularity and then fade from view. One week we see a cancer breakthrough; the next, we're reading about a possible "cure" for diabetes. One month we discover that "long telomeres" protect us and help us live a long and healthy life; the next month, that's debunked by a study that adds a horribly ironic twist: the longer your telomeres are, the greater your risk of developing cancer.

> **I get a lot of pushback from physicians saying, "Why would you want to burden a patient with that knowledge [of your ApoE type]?" I welcome that debate because it opens a discussion: Do you or do you not believe that this is a deterministic gene? If it's not deterministic, the next most important question is: Is there a manner in which you can alter the outcome? I believe the answer is emphatically yes: It's not deterministic, but it's risk-associated, and you can alter your trajectory. Therefore, how would you not want to know this?**
>
> —DR. PETER ATTIA

THE MEDICAL RESEARCH ESTABLISHMENT GIVETH—AND THEN TAKETH AWAY!

Afraid so. Some of the hype is probably traceable to sensationalized journalism. Health reporters, while generally knowledgeable about their niche, are under pressure to report on developments like these, as they attract "eyeballs." The reality of scientific research is that the development of interventions such as drugs and technologies can take a very long time to be thoroughly tested, and "early promise" doesn't always pan out in the long run.

That new Alzheimer's drug that showed promise in 2023? Well, in 2024, the FDA decided to hold off on giving it the green light until more tests were done on its safety and efficacy.

I SUPPOSE THAT'S TO BE EXPECTED, THOUGH, ISN'T IT?

Perhaps. But an unintended consequence of this rollercoaster experience is that people may become skeptical of new medical claims. Instead of greeting new developments with a sense of hope and possibility, people just shrug. Trust deteriorates.

Public skepticism probably reached new heights during the COVID pandemic, when the anti-vaxxers not only refused to get vaccinated but also politicized what should have been a routine intervention—an amazing scientific product that, while based on mRNA research stretching back to the 1960s, was developed as an effective vaccine in record time.

But earlier you asked about reducing risk. And that is a different kettle of fish, so to speak.

OKAY, SO HOW DO WE REDUCE OUR RISK OF CONDITIONS THAT MAY HAVE A GENETIC BASIS? ISN'T THAT PRETTY MUCH IMPOSSIBLE?

There's a statement from neurologist Richard Isaacson that I love: "Genes are not your destiny. You can win the tug of war against your genes." Now, he said this specifically referring to Alzheimer's disease, which, as we now know, can have a very strong genetic basis. But it does hold out hope that your future is not necessarily written in your DNA.

And Dr. Peter Attia clearly doesn't think all is lost just because you carry a gene that is associated with poor outcomes. I keep coming back to it because it's a good example, obviously. But again, Attia is a big promoter of knowing what version of the ApoE gene you have. His stance is not uncontroversial, as he himself admits in conversation with *The New York Times*. He says he's gotten a lot of pushback from doctors who wonder why he would burden patients with such anxiety-producing knowledge.

"I welcome that debate," he tells the reporter, "because it opens a discussion: Do you or do you not believe that this is a deterministic gene? If it's not deterministic, the next most important question is: Is there a manner in which you can alter the outcome?"

Attia himself believes that the answer to the second question is an emphatic "Yes." An adverse gene version can indicate risk, but, he says, "It's not deterministic. . .you can alter your trajectory. Therefore, how would you not want to know this?"

Unless your genetic makeup *determines* your fate—and science says this is usually not the case—then if you want to mitigate the risk, there are lifestyle choices that seem to be effective.

I guess one way of looking at this would be to think of a "bad" genome type as a heap of smouldering coals. You could walk away from the heat and hope it doesn't catch. This would be a passive response, but also a deliberate one: you would have chosen to turn away from the facts. You could also say, "To hell with it" and, figuratively speaking, throw a bunch of wood on the fire—by deciding to abuse substances, for example.

Or you could choose to spread the coals out, kick some dirt at the embers, and limit the chance for damage. That's the option that Dr. Attia is backing. And it's the one I would choose.

BUT WHAT CONCRETE STEPS CAN WE TAKE TO LIMIT THE NEGATIVE IMPACT THAT GENETICS COULD HAVE?

In my opinion, the cardinal rule of staving off decline and disease is to be mindful of our health—at all times and from as early an age as possible. We now know that you should know as much about yourself as you can, including whatever hard and fast data you can get. But really, the best weapon we have in the fight against any negative genetic predisposition is simple. It's exercise.

> **Count the number of times in human history when someone in the last decade of their lives said: 'I wish I had less muscle mass. I wish I was less strong.' The answer is zero.**
>
> —DR. PETER ATTIA, ON THE IMPORTANCE OF STRENGTH TRAINING IN STAVING OFF DECLINE

I'm not just talking about aerobic training, although that is definitely important. You also need to maintain your strength. It's something that I'm especially mindful of as a bodybuilder. People naturally lose muscle mass as they age; it's a process called sarcopenia. Just like with falls in older age, muscle loss is a much bigger problem than most people realize. In fact, the two are related: when you lose muscle strength, you also lose the ability to keep your balance—and that's one of the main reasons that many older people fall. It's also why they walk more slowly.

Need more convincing? Well, the fat and flab that replace muscle are associated with higher inflammation levels, lower testosterone and estrogen levels, insulin resistance and diabetes, and heart and lung disease. That's a lot of bad stuff that can be prevented with one simple action: strength training.

We'll talk more about this, and the kind of lifestyle changes we can make, a little later on.

WHAT ABOUT THE OPPOSITE? WE'VE BEEN TALKING ABOUT "BAD GENES," THE STUFF THAT CAN GO WRONG. WHAT ABOUT ALL THE WAYS THINGS CAN GO RIGHT? IS THERE A LONGEVITY GENE?

The short answer is "No." The better answer—as with so much to do with our health—is "It's complicated."

For example, even though, as we've seen, genes usually account for only about 25% of life expectancy, recent research shows that when you look at the top 10% longest-lived people, suddenly genetics seem to play a much bigger role. The researchers put it this way: "While human lifespan is only moderately heritable, 'getting old' runs in families."

In other words, the older a person gets, the more their genes get the credit. People whose parents live to 100 are more likely to reach the age of 70 in good health themselves, free of the typical age-related diseases. And people whose siblings live to 100 also tend to have long lives and stay disease-free longer than the average.

We can see some of this with the British royal family. People were awed when Queen Elizabeth II lived to the grand age of 96—but that was five years younger than her mother, who died at 101.

The U.S. National Library of Medicine sums it up by saying that the study of longevity genetics is "a developing science." That's probably the most cut-and-dried answer I can give you.

WHAT ABOUT RACE OR ETHNICITY? DO *THOSE* HAVE ANYTHING TO DO WITH LIVING LONGER, HEALTHIER LIVES?

Not generally—at least not when you factor out environmental influences.

SORRY, WHAT DO YOU MEAN?

Systemic racism is definitely a factor in healthcare delivery. Indigenous Canadians, for example, face discrimination in our country. The quality of health care they often receive can be inferior to what their non-native counterpart might receive, and their quality of life, along with their life expectancy, is often much lower. The same situation exists in other countries. In the United States, African Americans often face

When I was a kid, there were seven factories in town producing the cardboard, and they spewed their waste into the canal that runs through the village. We would breathe the terrible air. We would fish in the disgusting waters. In the summer, there would be a skim of foam about two feet thick floating on top of the water, due to the fact that that's where all the factories dumped their septic waste. The stench was unbearable. We lived right alongside the canal. The paint on our house would peel away, each and every year.

—JOHN BRINK, ON GROWING UP IN A TOXIC ENVIRONMENT

similar challenges.

Back to your original question: does race or ethnicity affect longevity? It definitely can. For example, through something called "founder mutations," a handful of ethnicities—namely, Ashkenazi Jews and people of Dutch, French Canadian, Icelandic, and Norwegian ancestry—have a significantly higher risk of carrying the BRCA1 and BRCA2 mutations that sharply increase the risk for breast cancer and several other cancers.

African-Americans have a higher likelihood than other ethnicities of getting sickle cell anemia, a disease that has very severe outcomes but may have arisen in tropical countries because it protects against malaria. Meanwhile, the genetic disease cystic fibrosis is found predominantly in White people of northern European descent.

So you can see that there are reasons you're asked about your family heritage at your doctor's office. But let's circle back to some good news: the mere presence of genes that are associated with negative health outcomes generally matters a whole lot less than the other two determinants: one, the world in which you live, and two, the way you choose to live in it.

We'll take a look at the first of these in the next chapter.

HIT OR MYTH?

Claim: Good genes usually determine your future health and wellness.

Studies on identical twins, who share nearly all the same genes, have shown just how much lifestyle behaviours influence brain health. In one of the largest studies of its kind, which looked at 392 pairs of twins aged 65 and up where one or both had Alzheimer's disease, genes accounted for 58 percent of a person's risk. The rest depended on lifestyle and environmental factors.

Verdict: Myth

CHAPTER FIVE

A BEAUTIFUL DAY IN THE NEIGHBOURHOOD?

It's not just who you are but where *you are that can make a difference in how long and how well you live. Your environment affects everything from your social safety nets and sense of community to the quality of health care you get. What impact does socioeconomic status have on longevity? Are there places where people age better and live longer? Does being a minority factor into lifespan and healthspan? Is social isolation a health problem in some societies? How do pollution and overcrowding affect health? And what about the impact of Covid-19, perhaps the most lethal environmental factor we've recently seen?*

I THINK THE TITLE OF THIS CHAPTER REFERS TO MR. ROGERS, YES? BUT I'M STILL A BIT CONFUSED WHAT THIS HAS TO DO WITH HEALTH AND HEALTHSPANS. CAN YOU EXPLAIN?

Absolutely. The point I'm trying to make is that your environment—your "neighbourhood," the setting where you reside—is a critical part of your life. The neighbourhood can be literal or metaphoric. It could encompass your apartment complex or the nation you call home—or even the ethnic group to which you belong. Your neighbourhood factors into the kind of life you'll end up leading, from how you interact with family and friends to whether your voice can be heard on political issues.

And for our purposes, it also affects whether you'll die young or old. It is likely more of a determinant of future health than genetics, which is something I've instinctively known since I was a child.

WHAT MADE YOU REALIZE THIS?

I was born in 1940, at the very start of World War II, and raised in a town called Sappemeer Oude Pekala, about 20 kilometres from the German border. As I discovered much later in life, being born into a time of war caused me to develop post-traumatic stress disorder, or PTSD. Today, almost 80 years later, I still shudder when I recall the thunderous sound of Allied warplanes flying in formation over our house. Remembering the sight of a horse-drawn cart piled high with dead bodies, a few stray legs dangling over the sides, still gives me a sick feeling.

There is no question in my mind that being born into this environment had a lasting traumatic effect. Psychologically, of course, but possibly even biologically.

HOW CAN SOMETHING THAT YOU EXPERIENCE IMPACT YOU BIOLOGICALLY?

All of the hard work paying off at another body-building competition.

Determined and feeling strong!

Erin Simpson, left, is responsible for making me fall in love with body-building

My day isn't complete without a hard training session at the gym, even in my mid-80s.

My personal trainer, Stefan Cloutier, and me in summer 2024.

Often times, my company supports fundraisers around the community such as The Inside Ride. This event required 60 minutes of cycling.

On my Harley Davidson motorcycle in Prince George, British Columbia.

BCABBA
© 2017 twixpix.com
VANCOUVER PRO/AM & EXPO
73
80

Gracing the stage at Provincials in British Columbia.

On stage in Vancouver at Body-Building Provincials.

Mike O'Hearn, the legend himself.

Erin Simpson, my dear friend and personal trainer who helped me take fitness, health, and wellness to the next level.

Practicing my posing before a body-building competition.

Pumping iron at Gold's Gym before an upcoming body-building competition.

The personification of Living Young, Dying Old.

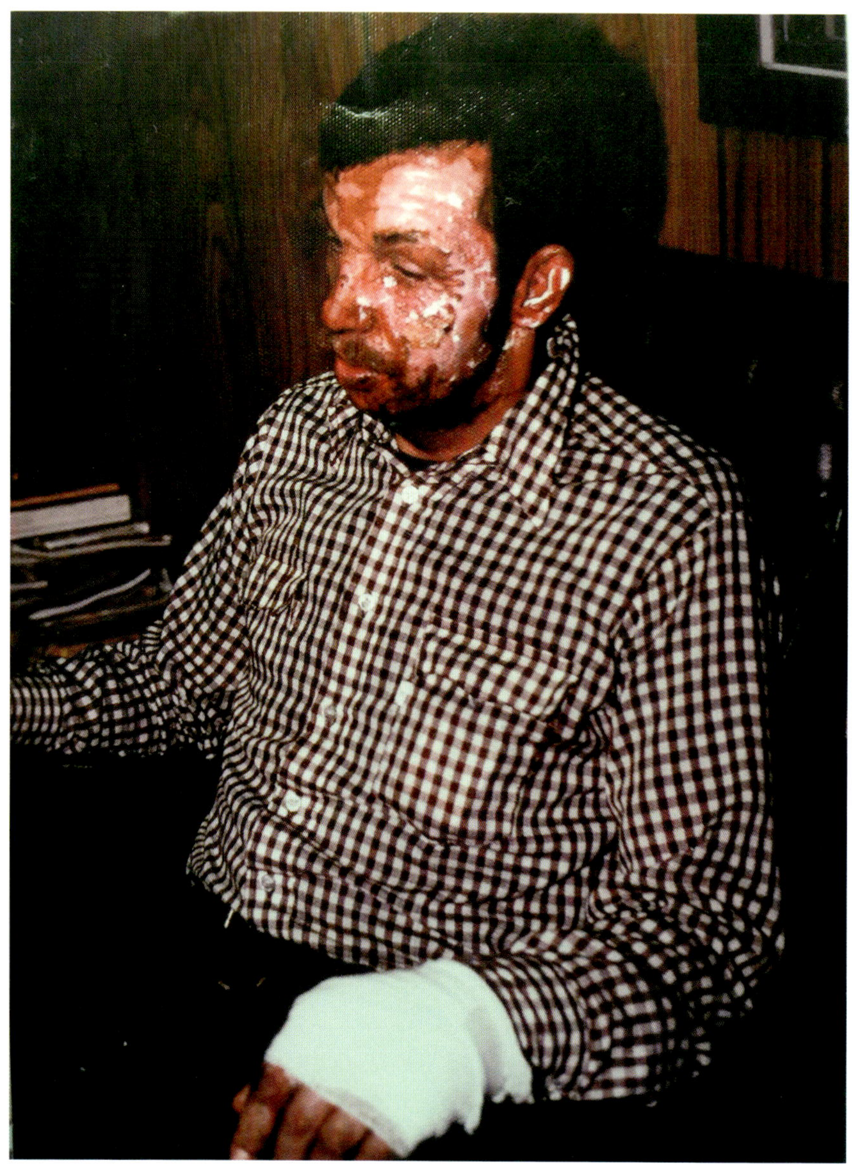

The result of a horrible burn, as discussed in the book's opening.

It's well-documented, actually. Remember our earlier discussion of epigenetics? Well, it turns out that the effects of trauma not only manifest physiologically but have the potential to alter our epigenetics—our "genetic expression." It can change who we are in ways that we pass along to our offspring. There is the potential to internalize trauma to the point where its effects essentially embed themselves. Some have said that this has occurred en masse. For example, persons of Jewish descent whose parents or grandparents endured the horrors of the Holocaust, or Indigenous survivors of residential schools, may carry or pass along the residue of those terrible events in their genes.

But in Oude Pekela, even when the war was finished, there were hazards lurking. And they were also related to environment. Let me set the scene for you.

Today, Oude Pekela is a village of about 8,000 people. Back when I lived there, it was home to a thriving cardboard-manufacturing industry. That industry has since collapsed, and in its wake there is resentment, and political populism—the typical outcomes of an afflicted population feeling they been given the short end of the stick and lashing out at whoever they can.

Anyway, when I was a kid, there were seven factories in town producing the cardboard, and they spewed their waste into the canal that runs through the village. That's not all: even the village sewage was dumped into the waters that crisscrossed the town. We would breathe the terrible air. In the summer, there would be a skim of foam about two feet thick floating on top of the water. The stench was unbearable.

My family lived right alongside the canal. Every year, the paint on our house would peel away.

Here's an interesting fact: my birthday is in November, right? By the time it rolled around each year, the canal would be frozen. For kicks, we'd cut a hole in the ice and then ignite the gas that escaped. It would literally catch fire! Thankfully, this is in the past. Oude Pekela is no longer an environmental disaster.

STILL, THAT'S UNBELIEVABLE!

Ah, but it's true. Really, I should be dead right now based on environmental factors alone. Let me tell you another story. When I first arrived in Canada, back in 1965, I started working at a Prince George sawmill called the Netherlands Overseas Mill. They were exporting unfinished wood to Holland, in lengths from 18 to 24 feet, and were attempting to compete with the Swedish products in that market. I mean, the strategy was flawed from the start: the transportation costs alone were significant.

But that's not my point. The thing is, the lumber was not dried out; instead, it was green! Because of the trees' natural moisture, the lumber was prone to molding. Obviously, they had to avoid this. So how did they do it? They dipped the wood in PCBs. And my job was to treat the wood with PCBs.

I'VE HEARD OF PCBS, BUT DON'T REALLY KNOW MUCH ABOUT THEM.

That's no surprise, since they've been banned internationally since 2001. PCB stands for polychlorinated biphenyls. They're carcinogenic, and they've been implicated in a wide variety of health issues, including immune, gastrointestinal, and even memory and attention difficulties. They used to be found in many industrial products. . .and the effects were felt mainly by those who were unlucky enough to encounter PCBs on a daily basis.

LIKE YOU.

Correct. For nine months straight, eight hours a day, every day, I'd be sloshing PCBs all over the wood. At the end of the day, I'd be soaked in PCBs, top to bottom. Even back then, however, we were somewhat aware of the danger. I mean, the stuff came in 45-gallon drums with a "dead head"—you know, the "poison skull" graphic?—on each barrel.

It's frightening as hell, of course, especially in retrospect. But this happens all the time. In the 1960s, you'd hear stories of kids playing in small hills of asbestos dust, or being greeted with a hug by their parents returning home from the asbestos plant, covered in perhaps one of the most dangerous materials ever produced. Whole families developed mesothelioma and died. And the stuff was everywhere: in vermiculite attic insulation, wrapped around pipes, incorporated into floor tiles, added to drywall.

It wasn't until maybe 20 years ago that we started understanding that if you ripped a house down or renovated an attic, you could be putting yourself in serious danger. Now, of course, you can't do a major reno or tear down an existing house without ensuring that any potential asbestos is removed by guys in full HAZMAT gear.

Oh, here's another lovely product. Do you recall the Shell "No-Pest Strips"?

I'M NOT SURE I DO. WHAT ARE THEY?

What *were* they. In the 1960s and 1970s, Shell produced an insecticide for in-home use. Basically, they were little cardboard containers that contained enough of the insecticide dichlorvos—a nerve poison—to kill any of the insects in your home. The problem, of course, is that *you* are also living there! After a young man died from possible exposure, Shell pulled the product in North America. But similar products, some of which are used to combat bedbug infestations, are still available for sale.

Look: when it comes to the environment, legislation often doesn't happen until it's too late. In the 1970s, before California implemented the Clean Air Act, smog in Los Angeles was so thick that air advisories were commonplace—much like many cities in India today. But people were suffering for a long time before anything was done. In 2015, the worldwide death toll from pollution was 9 million people. Imagine! But hey, you know, today most of those deaths are in non-Western countries. So, all good.

That's sarcasm, by the way.

I REALIZED THAT. BUT REALLY, THERE'S NOT TOO MUCH WE CAN DO ABOUT WHERE WE LIVE. IS THERE?

Well, I suppose you could always move to some place with cleaner air. Or if the danger was from what you do for a living, you could change jobs and pursue a career that didn't put you in contact with dangerous toxic materials.

Ultimately, though, knowledge is power. Collectively, change has happened because of this. Today in Los Angeles, even though the traffic snarls are as brutal as ever, the number of air advisories has dropped way off. California emissions standards resulted in the entire city "breathing easier." And the reason those emissions standards were implemented in the first place is that Californians took it upon themselves to elect politicians who were committed to dealing with the issue. So along with knowledge, political involvement is key. Californians, moved en masse to action, changed their world to be a better, healthier place.

But "environment" covers a lot of ground and encompasses much more than poison-spewing polluters or our ecological setting. It's much broader than that. Your environment consists of the world around you. Whether you live in a city or on a farm. Whether you have access to education and decent health care. Whether you're a member of the dominant ethnic group or a minority. Is poverty part of your picture? Well, that has an impact on healthspan too. In the U.S., even the political orientation of the state you live in can help or hurt. So, lots of different factors.

MY HEAD IS SPINNING. THERE'S ALMOST TOO MUCH TO TAKE IN.

There is a lot, it's true. Let's break it down, bit by bit. Let's talk about education first.

HOW IS EDUCATION PART OF THE ENVIRONMENT?

It exists outside your body, for one. It's an external factor, and accessing it depends on where you happen to be in the world. Now, this doesn't just mean "where you live." It also encompasses variables such as how accommodating the educational system is to your unique needs. And that can be dependent on time and place. For example, in Holland back in the 1940s and 1950s, there were no accommodations for anyone like me.

As I said, I have attention-deficit/hyperactivity disorder, or ADHD. It's significant. When I was younger, I could not read a book all the way through. When a teacher talked, I would fidget or carve little "roads" in the top of my wooden school desk. I failed Grade 3! Nobody does that. After failing Grade 7 three times, I finally gave up on formal education. I started working like an adult at the age of 13.

This is a bit of a sidebar, although not completely. The point I need to make is that your education level is directly related to health outcomes. Not for everybody—and not for me—but generally. For example, as of 2021, people in the U.S. with a four-year college degree could expect to live to 83 years old, an increase of four years from 1992.

WHAT ABOUT THOSE WITHOUT COLLEGE DEGREES?

Their experience was much different. In 1992, people without degrees could expect to live to around 77 years old—about two years fewer than their college-educated counterparts. By 2021, the non-degree group was only living to about 75. They were now living about eight and a half fewer years than people who had degrees, and the gap had increased. Their life expectancy had shrunk!

Yes, I'm talking about America, where the lack of health care can have a major effect. But it's true in Canada, too. In the past 20 years or so, the gap in life expectancy between educated and less educated people has grown from 6.5 years to nearly 8 years for men, and even more for women: from a difference of 5 years to nearly 7.

Some of this is likely related to another one of the above environmental factors: Poverty.

HOW DOES THAT INFLUENCE LONGEVITY?

It seems to be directly linked. A 2023 study in the *Journal of the American Medical Association* shows that poverty was responsible for over 180,000 deaths. Being poor killed more people in the U.S. than diabetes, drug overdoses, gun deaths, or suicide. Overall, it was the fourth-leading cause of death, after heart disease, cancer, and smoking. Now, the term "poverty" can cast a wide net; it's a catch-all that often includes other factors such as a higher incidence of smoking, substandard diet and nutrition, and, as we've already discussed, education.

> **The OCS has found that cigar-smoking, whiskey-swilling hundred-year-olds who effortlessly trek across mountain ranges to be myth.**
>
> —ONE CONCLUSION OF THE OKINAWA CENTENARIAN STUDY

As an interesting sidebar, in the U.S., a low-income person living in an affluent city with a highly educated population will do better than one living in a less affluent city with a less educated population. And for those who live in a so-called "red state," meaning where the Republican Party is usually in power, the situation might even be worse.

> **What's the downside of living with purpose, or pursuing daily activities that involve regular exercise? What's negative about not overeating, swapping out animal proteins for vegetables or having a strong sense of community and social connection? Maybe these ideas don't always translate into a long and healthy life in a direct cause-and-effect way, but they're actually a pretty good blueprint for living well.**
>
> —JOHN BRINK

WHY DO PEOPLE LIVE SHORTER LIVES IN THE "RED STATES"?

According to Nobel Prize-winning economist and *New York Times* columnist Paul Krugman, it has to do with government policy. Looking at life expectancy in different states together with their political leanings, he calculates that because of Republican politicians' reluctance to adopt mortality-lowering policies, the political orientation of the state a person lives in affects their longevity slightly more than their income does. Shocking, isn't it? He calls it "The Red State Death Trip."

ARE THERE AREAS WHERE PEOPLE DO BETTER, THOUGH? WHERE THE ENVIRONMENT IS A POSITIVE IN TERMS OF LIVING LONGER AND HEALTHIER LIVES?

Excellent question. There are—apparently. And they've received an amazing amount of coverage, especially lately. We mentioned them earlier. They're the so-called "Blue Zones."

The term and the concept were popularized by a *National Geographic* writer, Dan Buettner. Buettner first made his mark as a record-breaking transcontinental cyclist, so he knows a thing or two about healthy living, I'm sure.

But the phrase "Blue Zone" was actually coined in 2004 by a group of academic demographers looking into why villagers in a part of Sardinia, Italy, were living unusually long lives. The demographers drew blue circles around the area on their map—hence, "Blue Zone."

These researchers discovered that the village was home to a disproportionate number of people who lived to 100 years old or older. Even more unusually, many of them were men. They concluded, "Given the exceptionally high prevalence of male centenarians in the 'Blue Zone,' it is reasonable to assume that either the environmental characteristics or the genetic factors, or both, exert their favorable effect more strongly in men than in women."

So the whole "Blue Zone" term came from the use of a blue marker! But it does imply a calm, soothing life, doesn't it?

ACTUALLY, IT DOES. SO WHY DID IT BECOME SUCH A 'THING'?

That was mainly due to Dan Buettner's efforts. He expanded the concept, first in a 2005 *National Geographic* article and then in a 2008 book, *The Blue Zones: Lessons for Living Longer from the People Who've Lived the Longest.* Working with Michel Poulain, who had been part of the original demographic study, Buettner and his colleagues identified four more longevity hotspots, places where the locals appeared to be living longer and healthier lives than other people who lived in nearby areas.

Along with Nuoro Province, the original zone in Italy, the "Blue Zones" now include

- Ikaria, a Greek Island in the Aegean Sea
- Loma Linda, California
- Okinawa Prefecture, an island off Japan
- Nicoya Peninsula, Costa Rica

But Buettner wanted to go beyond just identifying places that had a higher number of folks living to 100 or longer. He wanted to find out what was *behind* their spectacular longevity and increased healthspans. In a way, like so many before him, he wanted to discover the Fountain of Youth.

WAS HE LOOKING FOR COMMONALITIES AMONG ALL THESE REGIONS? OR SOMETHING MORE?

What emerged was sort of a Venn diagram–like intersection of habits or circumstances. Some of these were socially based, and others had to do with diet and nutrition or exercise and attitude. In the end, he came up with a list of factors that may add up to longer, healthier lives.

There are quite a few, so let's go through them one by one.

First, Buettner found that "moving naturally" seemed to be a key component. That means, instead of "working out" or even "exercising" in the way that we tend to think of it, people in all five Blue Zones simply move around a lot for ordinary reasons, like herding their sheep, kneading their bread, and gardening.

Take the island of Sardinia, for example. Nuoro Province is a mountainous region, and many of the towns and villages are built on steep slopes. Just going about your day requires effort: a trip to and from the local market can be quite the workout. There's usually no time off from this, either. You don't get to wake up and say, "You know, I think I'll skip my aerobics class today." Your aerobics class is the way you get ingredients for lunch: there's no skipping it!

OKAY, SO "NATURAL MOVEMENT." WHAT ARE SOME OTHER FACTORS?

Buettner and friends also identified social connection, "family-first" relationships, and a sense of community belonging as key components. According to a summary of the research, "All but five of the 263 centenarians interviewed belonged to some sort of faith-based community." Now, I'm not a believer. In fact, I'm an agnostic. But I can see the value of close-knit communities consisting of people who share a common outlook.

As for the "family first" bit, this pertains to how the elderly in their communities are treated. In the Blue Zones, for the most part they don't warehouse their old folks in nursing homes. They take care of them at home, with the help of family and friends. As anyone who has ever worked in a nursing home can tell you, people who check in often don't have long before they check out, permanently.

The next factors are somewhat related. People in the Blue Zones cultivate and maintain a sense of purpose in their lives—what the Japanese call *ikigai*. In addition, they are also able to "downshift"—to decompress from stress—in ways that allow them to dodge the negative effects of stress-related inflammation. Remember my earlier mention of heart rate variability, which measures your nervous system's ability to shift from flight-or-flight mode to rest-and-digest mode? That ability, and all the health benefits that come from it, are at play here. As a National Institute of Health summary puts it, "Okinawans take a few moments each day to remember their ancestors; Adventists pray; Ikarians take a nap; and Sardinians do Happy Hour," where family and friends get together, often over a glass of wine.

I CAN GET BEHIND THE LAST ROUTINE. ANY OTHER FACTORS WE SHOULD KNOW ABOUT?

Another component part of living longer is diet. Now, of course what people eat differs from Zone to Zone. But in most cases, Buettner found that a *plant-based diet* was key and that meat was eaten sparingly. Of course, this dovetails with much that we've learned about the benefits of incorporating more vegetables into our diets. Okinawans have another principle relating to diet: the 80% Rule.

WHAT'S THE "80% RULE"?

Okinawans stop eating when they're only about fourth-fifths full. They call this practice *hara hachi bu*, and it means that they end up eating far fewer calories than the average Westerner—only about 1,200 calories a day, compared to the American average of 3,600. If, as animal studies suggest, calorie restriction consistently slows the aging process, the 80% Rule could be a major factor behind Okinawans' longevity. Plus, the order of their meals is different from the way many of us eat. Their smallest meal of the day takes place in late afternoon or early evening, and they don't indulge after this.

And then there's wine. With the exception of the Seventh Day Adventist community in Loma Linda, who for religious reasons don't partake, the people in the rest of the Blue Zones drink moderately.

BUT I THOUGHT THAT THE NEW SCIENCE AROUND DRINKING HAD DETERMINED THAT NO AMOUNT OF ALCOHOL IS CONSIDERED SAFE?

You're right: alcohol is now being treated by much of the medical community as a toxic substance, and the International Agency for

Research on Cancer has classified it as a Group 1 carcinogen since 1988. In case you're wondering, that's the same group as cigarettes, radiation, and asbestos.

In Canada, the official "low-risk drinking" guidelines are no more than 15 standard drinks a week for men, 10 for women. But there is new pushback on even these modest amounts. The Canadian Centre on Substance Use and Addiction defines "low-risk drinking" as *one to two* drinks a week. Health Canada hasn't officially adopted these standards as of the writing of this book, but they could.

I'm raising this not because I'm a killjoy, but because there is some controversy about the Blue Zones and some of the conclusions that have been drawn from the research. According to the debunking website Science-Based Medicine, there could be "fraud and error" behind some of the longevity claims. "Record-keeping has been deficient in many of those areas; systematic verification of age has been practiced only recently and only in some parts of the world," they write. "People may be confused with parents and grandparents who had the same name. People can lie."

Why would someone lie about when they were born? Pension fraud, for one. If you add 20 years to your birth date, you're basically jumping the queue for receiving government benefits. And remember: if someone is 100 years old in 2024, they were born in 1924. That's well before most countries initiated a system of verifiable records. So this kind of fraud would be fairly easy to pull off.

There have also been some critical examinations of the science behind Buettner's work. The links between lifestyle factors and living long, healthy lives are, in some cases, hard to prove. The claim that Okinawa is a Blue Zone is also under attack—even by Dan Buettner, oddly enough. He now says that because of the impact of a Western diet, Okinawans have recently developed higher rates of obesity and diabetes, leading him to disqualify the area.

OKAY, BUT THAT SEEMS TO IMPLICATE SHIFTING LIFESTYLE FACTORS—NOT NECESSARILY DISQUALIFY THE WHOLE THING!

Correct. But some think there is an inherent problem with the connections made. For example, Saul Newman, an Oxford academic, researched newspaper articles about people who were living extraordinarily long lives, and claimed that only a small percentage, less than 15%, had a birth certificate, "even in countries with 95% coverage." His general take? That these supercentenarians are either mistaken about when they were born or they're frauds.

Then again, there are others who line up on the opposite side and buy into the Blue Zones as a way to discover the habits that can help us age better. I'm not in a position to determine which camp is right. But I needed to throw it out there: just because something hits a public nerve doesn't mean it's solid science.

As a basic blueprint for living a healthy life, though, I don't find anything wrong with the Blue Zones theory. What's the downside of living with purpose, pursuing daily activities that involve regular movement, eating moderately, swapping out animal proteins for vegetables, and having a strong sense of community and social connection?

Maybe these ideas don't always translate into a long and healthy life in a direct cause-and-effect way, but they seem like a pretty good blueprint for living well. That's important, and many would tend to agree. And that's probably why there's an interest in creating Blue Zones from scratch.

HOW DO YOU CREATE A BLUE ZONE?

There's a project underway in a Brooklyn neighbourhood that's giving it a go. East New York is one of the poorest areas in metropolitan

New York City, and that's where they're experimenting with a new development. According to *The New York Times*, it will consist of a 2.5-million-square-foot affordable housing project, at a cost of about USD $1.2 billion, paid for mainly by the state government. Seeking to duplicate the close-knit community and opportunity for natural movement of the Blue Zones, it will feature plenty "of walking paths, recreation areas and facilities intended to foster community, as well as a farm for fresh vegetables."

Will it work? We'll have to see.

WHAT OTHER SYSTEMIC ISSUES MIGHT AFFECT HEALTH AND LONGEVITY?

Race and ethnicity, for example. Marginalized communities often receive inadequate care, and that's pretty much a given. But even living in a society where your day-to-day life is affected by racism can lead to dramatically reduced lifespans. For example, in one mainly African American part of Oakland, California, the residents' average lifespan is 15 years lower than in areas dominated by well-off whites just north of the neighbourhood.

HOW IS THAT POSSIBLE? AND ANYHOW, WOULDN'T IT BE BECAUSE OF ECONOMIC DIFFERENCES, NOT RACISM DIRECTLY?

I wouldn't rule out the latter. But University of Michigan public-health researcher Arline Geronimus believes that the premature ageing due to racism also happens at a biological and even cellular level, through African Americans suffering the continual, inflammation-causing stress of racism. Geronimus calls it "weathering," because the chronic stress literally wears on the body's organs, hormones, and cells the way the beating sun does on the paint of a house, leading to the same kind of rapid ageing.

Which raises a question: is this a transgenerational epigenetic event, a heritable result of ongoing trauma? Is a shorter lifespan due to trauma literally passed on from one generation to another? Again, I'm not an expert, but epigenetic transmission is real, and this possibility certainly wouldn't be beyond the pale.

ARE THERE ANY OTHER SOCIAL FACTORS WE SHOULD BE AWARE OF?

Yes: as I mentioned before, social isolation and loneliness play a major part in lifespan and healthspan. And the problem goes beyond the developed world: the U.S. surgeon general notes that the 25% figure for people suffering from social isolation is similar in all areas of the world. In 2023, the World Health Organization declared that loneliness was "a pressing global threat" and created an international commission to study the problem.

It's not just about a lot of people feeling sad and lonely, either. Living a disconnected life can increase your risk of dementia by 50% and your risk of stroke or heart disease by 30%.

It's significant. But we're forgetting one of the most destructive environmental factors, one that just recently caused life expectancies to dip dramatically in many countries around the globe.

And that's Covid-19.

In Canada, the novel coronavirus was responsible for more than 16,000 deaths in 2020. That same year, it was the third leading cause of death nationally after cancer and heart disease, respectively. It trimmed about a half a year from our life expectancy rates, so those who were born in 2020 could expect to live to 81.7 years of age, as opposed to 82.3 in 2019. That's the most significant dip in life expectancy since 1921—which, of course, was the year that deaths from the 1918-1919

Spanish flu pandemic started showing up in life-expectancy figures.

The U.S. fared worse. With President Trump refusing to implement a science-based COVID policy, more than 350,000 Americans died of COVID in 2020, and 1.1 million had died by the middle of 2023.

By contrast, most of the Scandinavian countries—Denmark, Finland and Norway—did well, with no significant drop in life expectancy in 2020, the year we were all hit hard. Sweden was the outlier. With a government that believed in "herd immunity" and refused to implement lockdown measures when most other countries were, the country had more than 9,000 COVID deaths in 2020, compared to under 500 in neighbouring Norway, and had reached almost 15,000 COVID deaths by the next summer, the second-highest per capita in the region of Scandinavia and Eastern Europe.

YES, BUT HOW IS A "DISEASE" AN ENVIRONMENTAL THING?

Think about it. Covid-19 isn't like cancer, diabetes, or heart disease, whose effects are normally confined to the afflicted. No, the transmissibility of Covid-19 makes it much different. The virus spreads through contact with others—with those who inhabit the same space as you do.

So, is all lost, then? Of course not. It's true: genetics and environment both play significant roles in how long we can expect to live a healthy life. But the biggest determinant by far—and the greatest opportunity, as well—is found in the way we live our lives. Beyond all doubt, when it comes to extending our healthspans, lifestyle can be our greatest enemy. And, as we'll see in the next chapter, it can also be the key to unlocking a longer, more rewarding life.

CHAPTER SIX

YOU DO YOU: LIFESTYLE AND LONGEVITY

More than any other factor, adjusting your lifestyle choices gives you the most bang for the healthspan buck. So what, exactly, is a good strategy for healthy living? What role does exercise play? What about diet and nutrition? Are supplements something we should consider? Does attitude play a role? Is retirement a desirable goal or the first step on the road to decline? And why is the "80/20 Rule" an integral part of keeping yourself on the right track and learning to live well for longer?

FRANKLY, THIS IS THE CHAPTER I'VE BEEN WAITING FOR.

I'm glad to hear it. Of the three determining forces, lifestyle is way more of a factor than genetics or environment. As we've learned, however, your life is not some predetermined set of days. Even though your genetic history is obviously important, for the vast majority of people it isn't like a time bomb set to go off once you reach a certain age. In the same way, environment doesn't necessarily *determine* your healthspan. The main reason, of course, is that when it comes to the longevity game, what you do is far more important than who you are (genetics) or where you happen to be in the world (environment).

Now that said, don't misread me: I'm not saying that genetics or environment are unimportant. What I believe is that it is often up to the individual to create a path forward that can maximize healthspan, even if they have drawn a shorter straw in terms of genetics or environment.

We can't overcome everything. But for most of us, adjusting the way we live—how we eat, move, think, and believe—can be the basis for a powerful life-extension philosophy. It is something that, again in the words of JFK, can "add years to your life, and life to your years."

OKAY. WHERE DO WE START?

Let's begin by taking a look at what we put into ourselves. This is a surprisingly large category. Do you smoke? How much booze do you drink? Fancy a bong hit to unwind after a long day? Do you snack? On what? Like most North Americans, do you get the bulk of your nutrition from processed foods?

THAT'S A LOT TO TAKE IN.

So to speak! So to start, let's go shopping.

> **What most people don't realize is that food is not just calories: It's information. It actually contains messages that communicate to every cell in the body.**
>
> —DR. MARK HYMAN

The first misstep that most of us make is going to the grocery store and coming home with all the wrong things. Although this is very basic, the first thing you should never do is shop on an empty stomach. If you're hungry, you tend to gravitate toward the kind of foods that give instant gratification. Most of these are "fun" to eat: potato chips, pizzas, frozen kung pao chicken entrées, whatever. The list is long and, for many, tempting. But the reality is that a lot of these foods should come with warnings equivalent to the ones found on cigarette packages.

Some of these convenient, good-tasting foods are killing us. The list of chronic health conditions associated with highly processed food is long and terrifying. We can start with diabetes, some cancers, and obesity and the poor health outcomes that go hand in hand. Then there are the cognitive issues, such as dementia, that researchers are now connecting to a diet high in processed foods and low in nutrients and fibre.

BUT AREN'T MOST FOODS WE BUY PROCESSED IN SOME WAY? I MEAN, AREN'T MIXED NUTS A PROCESSED FOOD?

Yes, you're correct. And your underlying assumption is also correct: not all processed foods are automatically poor choices. For example, some brands of roasted nuts would likely be considered "minimally processed." Other items, like canned tomatoes or chickpeas, for example, also undergo processing. I mean, they come in cans, right? But these

> **If you keep good food in your fridge, you will eat good food.**
>
> —ERRICK MCADAMS, PERSONAL TRAINER

are still recommended by dieticians and are usually a better choice than a premade pasta sauce or commercially made hummus.

So yes, there is a pecking order. But did you know that Canadians and Americans get 50% and 60% of their calories, respectively, from food that is not just processed, but highly processed? That should definitely give us pause. From luncheon meats to many fully prepared and prepackaged container meals, *highly* processed foods are everywhere.

But I digress. Let's hit the grocery store.

OKAY. WHAT DO I NEED TO KNOW TO GO SHOPPING WITH YOU?

I do most of the grocery shopping for our house. It's something that I do regularly and enjoy. Over time, I've come up with two basic rules. This first is: Avoid the interior aisles. This is where you'll find many of the processed foods. It's a simple but effective approach, but we don't have to elevate it to an orthodoxy. If you need something food-related from the interior aisles, go for it. Oils, dried spices, canned salmon, frozen fruits and vegetables—while fresh and natural alternatives exist, these are compromises that can easily be made.

Remember, though, that almost everything you buy that comes in a package or a can is in that form for convenience. If you have the time and the inclination, you could pretty much avoid buying even "acceptable" processed foods. Take pasta sauce, for example. The ones you'll find on supermarket shelves—again, in the interior aisles—often contain added sugars and preservatives. In fact, the nutrition-tracking website Eat This, Not That! notes that pasta sauces from one famous brand contain more sugar than a bowl of Froot Loops.

YOU MAKE YOUR OWN PASTA SAUCE FROM SCRATCH, THEN?

No, I don't. Then again, I rarely eat pasta, because refined flour isn't something I want to eat on any kind of regular basis. But added sugar is something I avoid like the plague.

WELL, SURE, WE KNOW THAT SUGAR CAN MAKE YOU GAIN WEIGHT.

It's not just that. There's a growing body of evidence that implicates added sugar in other poor health outcomes.

YOU SAY "*ADDED* SUGAR." WHY THE DISTINCTION?

Added sugar, as opposed to sugars that naturally occur. Because refined sugar is often added to foods to make them taste better, and it can be difficult to tease out how much you're actually consuming; everything from ketchup to cured meats can contain added sugar. And yes, you're right: obesity can result from ingesting too much. But other issues can be related to excess added sugar consumption, too, like diabetes and, as we now know, overall cardiovascular health.

> **To lengthen thy life, lessen thy meals.**
>
> —BENJAMIN FRANKLIN

Just stay away from added sugars. My two cents!

ANY OTHER TIPS FOR WHAT TO AVOID WHEN WE'RE OUT SHOPPING?

Absolutely. This one goes hand in hand with my previous principle and is something you'll see dieticians and nutritionists advising: if something includes an ingredient that is exceptionally long or difficult to pronounce, you might want to leave it out of your cart.

Fancy a plate of monosodium glutamate? Butylated hydroxyanisole? Hydrolyzed vegetable protein? Sodium aluminum phosphate? Would you like some fries with that? (Skip those, too, unless you're in the mood for sodium acid pyrophosphate, sodium bicarbonate, modified cornstarch, dextrose, dried torula yeast, xanthan gum, and sodium acid pyrophosphate.)

Sometimes cutting through the chaff to get to the wheat can be difficult, according to Daryl Bouchard, a holistic nutritionist who in 2023 was a guest on my podcast, *On the Brink*.

WHAT'S A "HOLISTIC NUTRITIONIST"?

In a nutshell, it's someone who helps educate people about nutrition, but by emphasizing more of a natural approach to diet. They can also help guide us through the maze of good, poor, or completely misleading information.

SO HOW DO WE NAVIGATE THROUGH THIS MAZE? HOW CAN WE AVOID BAD ADVICE AND BECOME BETTER INFORMED?

I'm going to let Daryl answer this one:

> What I try to teach my clients is to prioritize whole food as much as possible. If it comes from the ground and roams the plains as freely as possible, and we're consuming this as the largest part of our diet, then we're off to a great start.
>
> Anything that comes from a box, a can, a jar, or a bag, proceed

> with caution. I educate my clients on how to read food labels, decipher marketing tactics, know what's in their food products. When we're aware of what's in our food, then we can make a mindful decision as to how much of that food product we want to consume, and we no longer fall victim to mindless consumerism.

Her number-one recommendation? If someone feels lost or overwhelmed, seek out a nutrition program that aligns with the path that they want to be on. Or hire a reputable health practitioner—Daryl Bouchard, for example!—to help get started. It's a minefield of unpronounceable additives and preservatives out there. As Daryl says, proceed with caution.

OKAY, THOSE MULTISYLLABIC INGREDIENTS DEFINITELY FREAK ME OUT. ARE THEY TYPICAL OF PROCESSED FOODS?

Not all of them. I recently read the ingredients list on a can of organic pumpkin. Do you know what was in it?

I'M AFRAID TO ASK.

Organic pumpkin.

WELL, THAT'S GOOD!

Yes, it is. So again, use my grocery-shopping hack as a guide only, not like it's The Bible. Doing most of your shopping in the outside aisles and reading the ingredients list will help you stay away from some of the dodgier foods. Be aware, though, that some foods even in the outside aisles are unhealthy. For example, the deli-meat section is often on the periphery. And the link between poor health outcomes and processed meats is very well established.

My point is, just be aware. Also, a lot of that stuff is beyond processed, or even highly processed: it's *ultra*-processed.

CAN WE GET A DEFINITION?

Eurídice Martínez Steele, a University of Sao Paulo food researcher, defined it this way in a *New York Times* article: "Ultra-processed foods include ingredients that are rarely used in homemade recipes—such as high-fructose corn syrup, hydrogenated oils, protein isolates, and chemical additives." This also includes things like "colors, artificial flavors, sweeteners, emulsifiers and preservatives."

> **Sitting is the new smoking.**
>
> —MAYO CLINIC PROFESSOR OF MEDICINE JAMES LEVINE (ATTRIB.)

This lines up with my rule to avoid buying items with unpronounceable ingredients. The same piece mentions that ultra-processed foods make up a whopping 70% of the packaged foods sold in the U.S. These foods often contain dangerously high levels of salt, sugar, and fat.

An additional danger is that if you eat these foods in a fast-food setting, you probably won't have any idea what you you're eating—unless you go online and look up the ingredients list. That's exactly what I did with the recipe for McDonald's famous fries, and here's what I found:

> *Potatoes, High oleic low linolenic canola oil and/or canola oil, Hydrogenated soybean oil, Natural flavour (vegetable source), Sugars (dextrose), Sodium acid pyrophosphate (maintain colour), Citric acid (preservative), Dimethylpolysiloxane (antifoaming agent).*

Cooked in vegetable oil (high oleic low linoleic canola oil and/or canola oil, corn oil, soybean oil, hydrogenated soybean oil, citric acid, dimethylpolysiloxane)

Even the ingredients list for the *salt* they use on the fries is, um, "complicated": salt, silicoaluminate, sugar (dextrose), potassium iodide.

I'm pretty sure French fries are basically potatoes, oil, and salt. This is the ingredients list for the fries at western U.S. fast-food chain In-N-Out Burgers, which goes to show that if a chain really wants to serve fast food that's not full of the food-processing equivalent of embalming fluid, they can do it.

OKAY, BUT WHAT'S THE DOWNSIDE OF EATING ULTRA-PROCESSED FOODS?

Eating ultra-processed food has been implicated in obesity, diabetes, and some cancers, as well as depression, anxiety, and even cognitive decline. Now, as with many scientific issues, these foods haven't yet been proven to cause the outcomes—but a 2024 overview of studies showed that there was "consistent" evidence linking ultra-processed foods to 32 negative health outcomes. Within this, the scientists classified evidence as "convincing" for a link between ultra-processed foods and a 50% higher risk of death from cardiovascular disease, a 48 to 53% higher risk of anxiety and other mental disorders, and a 12% higher risk for developing type 2 diabetes. They classified the evidence as "highly suggestive" for links between these foods and a 21% higher risk of death from any cause, as well as raised risk for obesity, sleep problems, and depression.

The food-processing industry has seen the writing on the wall, and, as you might expect, they don't like how it reads. The industry has pushed back, and we will likely see a lot more of this— especially since several countries, Canada included, are now warning of the possible dangers of a processed-food–heavy diet.

We've seen this sort of slow-moving thought evolution before. I'm not drawing a direct comparison, but in the 1950s, there was very little awareness of the health effects of smoking cigarettes. You can see how that turned out.

The main point is to have a good idea of what you should and shouldn't be putting into your body. I think we can all agree that smoking is incredibly damaging to health. Highly processed foods are starting to look like a very bad idea. And as we've already said, there's also a growing body of evidence that drinking alcohol, even any amount, is harmful. So, another habit to reconsider.

WE'VE SPENT A FAIR BIT OF TIME TALKING ABOUT WHAT YOU DON'T PUT INTO YOUR BODY. MAYBE IT'S TIME FOR US TO TALK ABOUT WHAT YOU *DO*?

Absolutely. And you're correct: focusing on what we shouldn't do is always a bit of a dangerous game. It can be overwhelming, and that's never a good motivator for change. If you get to the point where people just throw up their hands and say, "Well, everything I do is harmful!" that's not good. And it's not what I'm trying to achieve.

I do want to emphasize that there are costs associated with our behaviours. We are free to make choices, and if those choices ultimately are not in our best interests, well, that's the cost of being an adult armed with free will. Ultimately, though, we have to reckon with the consequences. To put it

> **Physical fitness is not only one of the most important keys to a healthy body, it is the basis of dynamic and creative intellectual activity.**
>
> —JOHN F. KENNEDY

Biblically, we reap what we sow.

You *can* change bad habits and poor patterns. You have it within your grasp to make the kind of lifestyle changes that will increase your healthspan. This is good news!

OKAY, SO HOW DO WE START? WHAT DO YOU EAT?

I eat simply. You might even say my diet is boring. But in my opinion, "boring" is good! On the days I work out, I'll have lunch around 12:30. Now to some people, my "lunch" might seem a stretch: I'll do a protein shake from Gold's Gym, the one with high protein and low carbs and sugars. On my non-workout days I'll have a bowl of vegetarian soup or, occasionally, grab a sandwich from Starbucks.

Between 5 and 6 p.m. I'll go out for dinner, which is almost always the same: a spinach salad, usually with grilled chicken breast, and occasionally a cup of clam chowder on the side. Then I'll usually go back to the office and put in another couple of hours. I'm in bed by 9:00, usually.

No red meat. No alcohol. No dairy aside from cheese, and then only occasionally. So: very simple and very predictable. I'm not a "foodie."

Now, if I'm within a month or so of a bodybuilding competition, I'll alter my diet. During this period, protein is critical, but so is ensuring that I'm eating enough food to help repair my muscles after workouts. Frequency of meals is also important when it comes to proper recovery and muscle growth. All this matters.

But in terms of longevity, it's not just what you eat or what you don't eat—it's *how much*. And overeating is something I definitely avoid. Just like the Okinawans, I suppose.

WELL, SURE. IF YOU OVEREAT, YOU GAIN WEIGHT. AND THAT'S NOT GOOD, RIGHT?

There's a bit more to it than that. For some time now, there has been research into the benefits of a calorie-restricted diet. As long as it doesn't veer into extremes, eating less on a regular basis may translate to a longer, healthier life. Both short-term and longer-term "caloric restriction" have been linked with measurable improvements. In *Outlive*, Peter Attia devotes an entire chapter to the positive health effects of eating less—and of fasting, which he also believes can help "reboot" our physiologies.

Most of the supporting studies, as usual, were done on lab rodents. "The results have been remarkably consistent," Attia writes. "Studies dating back to the 1930s have found that limiting caloric intake can lengthen the lifespan of a mouse or rat from anywhere from 15% to 45%, depending on the age of onset and degree of restriction."

The association between eating less and living longer was also observed in humans in real life, as opposed to clinical trials. As Dr. Michael Greger notes in *How Not to Age*, a blockade on food supplies to Denmark during World War I was accompanied by a 34% reduction in the death rates. Likewise, in World War II, the war I was born into, Greger writes that "a 20% drop in calories was accompanied by a 30% drop in death rates."

Fascinating! And, pardon the pun, food for thought.

YOU DIDN'T MENTION BREAKFAST. DO YOU SKIP IT?

Not at all. Most days, after getting up around 5:30 a.m., I'll have three or four boiled eggs and a whole avocado for breakfast.

EGGS? AVOCADOS? ONE IS ASSOCIATED WITH HIGH CHOLESTEROL, AND THE OTHER IS FULL OF FAT!

First off, "fat" is a broad term, and not all fats are bad for you.

Nuts, fish, and olive oil, for example, are all major components of the Mediterranean diet, which is pretty much always touted as an example of how to eat smartly. Avocados are full of anti-inflammatories and antioxidants. A 2022 large-scale cohort study published in the *Journal of the American Heart Association*, taking place over a three-decade span, found that eating more avocado was associated with a lower risk of both cardiovascular and coronary heart disease, and that swapping out some fat-containing foods for avocado lowered the risk of cardiovascular disease. That's pretty solid.

As for the egg controversy…really, the best science now says that dietary cholesterol, which is different from serum cholesterol, is not a huge issue for most. I have no issues with high cholesterol at all, so I'm comfortable with my pattern of egg consumption.

But I also make use of vitamins and other supplements.

DO THESE REALLY HELP?

I believe they do. And it's not just me. My doctors also believe in them. To make it easier, instead of rooting around in a bunch of bottles every day, I just reach for Metagenics' Wellness Essentials blister pack and it's done. It's very convenient, and convenience is king.

WHAT'S IN THE BLISTER PACK? WHAT ARE YOU ACTUALLY TAKING?

There's a lot packed into those packs, which claim to improve heart, immune, and neurological health, as well as mood. The packets include vitamins A, C, D, E, K and B12, along with the B vitamins thiamin, riboflavin, and niacin, the essential fatty acids DHA and EPA, minerals like magnesium and calcium, and a long list of plant-based micronutrients, like bioflavonoids and chlorogenic acid.

It's become a habit, so I really don't think too much about it. Get up, have breakfast, do the blister pack.

I also do a weekly IV drip with a booster of vitamins and supplements. It's ease of use that's the draw: I'm there, I sit for about an hour, and it's done. In the process, I ensure that I'm doing what I can to address any nutrient deficiencies and am also helping cleanse my body of toxins and free radicals. I've also found that it increases my energy levels and promotes relaxation. All good.

In addition, I also take regular injections of Plaquex®, which helps to promote better circulation and reduce inflammation. It's a strictly proactive measure, but my naturopathic doctor feels that the potential benefits are significant. It takes about 90 minutes, so I sit back, relax, and let it do its magic.

ISN'T THERE A FAIR BIT OF CONTROVERSY ABOUT SUPPLEMENTS? I'M SURE I'VE COME ACROSS NEWS ARTICLES THAT CLAIM THEY DON'T PROVIDE ANY BENEFIT WHATSOEVER.

There's some very solid science behind supplements. And some extremely solid scientists, too. Take Bruce Ames, for example. Here's a guy who has the U.S. 1998 National Medal of Science and spent the years 1976 to 1982 as a board member of the U.S. National Cancer Advisory Board. He's the person behind the "Ames Test," which is used to identify whether chemicals pose a health risk to humans. He's a serious individual, and in the latter part of his career, he turned his sharp eye to the processes involved in ageing.

He's now 95 years old, and in good health. And he believes that one day we'll be able to have our blood analyzed and the results will enable us to come up with a personalized supplement "cocktail" that will dramatically slow the ageing process. Until that time, though, he says that taking vitamins—41 vitamins and minerals, actually—will go a long way in helping keep people healthy as they age.

> **I have chosen to be happy because it is good for my health.**
>
> —VOLTAIRE

Ames bases this claim on something he calls "the triage theory." Basically, the theory says that when our body gets low on certain micronutrients, it has to "triage," or prioritize, the limited supply of that nutrient, just like a nurse at the desk of the ER decides which patients need to see the doctor most urgently. Should the body use the nutrient to fix immediate issues or to keep everything running smoothly? As a 2018 article in *Inverse* puts it, "Ames believes that if the body is always well-supplied, it should never have to make that choice."

Now, Ames does add that if you're eating right, you're covering a lot of the bases already. But if there's no harm, then where's the foul? As long as you're composing your supplement intake with the guidance of a doctor who knows what they're doing, in my opinion the downside is very limited.

WHAT ELSE IS KEY?

Well, we already have a magic pill. If you take it daily, and in the correct doses, it will extend your healthspan. It will make you feel better, allow you to resist disease, and fight the inexorable effects of ageing. It has been shown to reduce cognitive impairment. It will help you to avoid having an accidental fall, and if you do have one, it will go a long way toward allowing you to recover fully.

THAT SOUNDS AMAZING, ALMOST LIKE SNAKE OIL! WHY HAVEN'T I HEARD OF THIS BEFORE? SIGN ME UP!

Not so fast. The magic pill is *exercise.*

OH. HMM.

That doesn't excite you? Maybe you should reconsider. More and more, we're discovering that keeping fit and active is absolutely the number-one way that you can extend your healthy life. There are vast numbers of studies confirming the health benefits of exercise. And there's a rapidly growing amount of research telling us what we should instinctively know: that being inactive is the worst thing you can do.

Have you heard the phrase "Sitting is the new smoking"? It's not hyperbole. Sitting too much is a health hazard. It's also an epidemic, as the nature of how we spend our days has changed dramatically over the years. Did you know that "sedentary jobs"—that's where we're at our desks for a large part of the day—have increased by over 80% since 1950?

According to a 2023 research study, the more time you spend on your butt, the more you put yourself at risk—and the risks show up in places that you might not expect. As an article in the *South China Morning Post* summed it up, "The risk for dementia rose 8 per cent for being sedentary for 10 hours, 63 per cent for 12 hours, and 321 per cent for 15 hours."

Imagine. In your body, everything is interconnected. You are a system. And the only way to maintain that system is through what evolution designed our bodies to do: move, lift, play, walk.

As the Nike ad says, *Just do it.* Or to put it another way: "Move it or lose it." Because the less you move, the less fit you'll become. The less fit you become, the less inclined you'll be to move, which in turn leads to being even less fit, and so on. You see how this works?

OKAY, BUT WHAT DO *YOU* DO? CAN YOU RUN DOWN YOUR EXERCISE ROUTINE?

Sure.

First, my regular workout revolves around a trainer: having someone to guide and encourage me helps to keep me accountable. Personally, I like to have a goal in mind, one that I'm working towards—a bodybuilding competition, for example. But goals are personal, of course, and not everyone wants to engage in competitive bodybuilding. My goal is mine alone. Other goals could range from rejigging your lifestyle—better sleep or cutting down on booze—to using the stairs instead of an elevator. Start small, and make sure that whatever goal you choose is attainable.

HOW OFTEN ARE YOU AT THE GYM?

My goal is always between 5 and 10 hours a week, but this can increase while I'm getting closer to a bodybuilding competition. In the off-season, I'm consistently at the gym for three days a week with my trainer, but I ramp this up to five days a week when we get closer to competitions.

My workouts consist of targeting various muscle groups, and I'll change it up throughout the week. One day I'll concentrate on my chest, the next it might be legs, followed by core and cardio on the other days. Then my trainer might have me wrap up the week with some strength training that includes shoulders, biceps, and triceps. The time I spend on each exercise varies, but I'll often spend an entire one-hour training session on a single muscle group.

In terms of bench pressing or any other strength-training exercise, I don't do "one-max reps," so I don't know the maximum amount I can bench press. And I'm not really interested in knowing, either. Instead, I focus on finding the right weight where I can complete, say, 8 to 12 repetitions before "muscle failure." Once I have the target weight, I'll do three or four sets. For toning purposes, I'll lift lighter weights but perform more reps—around 16 to 24, generally.

Again, I've always found a personal trainer invaluable, but at my gym I also see a lot of friends or couples working out, and it seems they use the gym as a social occasion or to share the passion of moving their bodies together. Still others may be there to blow off stress: there's nothing like a good dopamine-inducing workout to shed tension and anxiety. I mean, there's a reason dopamine is called "the happy hormone."

DO YOU DO AEROBIC TRAINING AT ALL? IF YES, WHAT DO YOU DO TO GET YOUR HEART RATE UP?

I can't emphasize enough the importance of a solid warm-up, which helps get the heart rate up and properly prepares you for the hard work ahead. Before a typical strength-training workout with my personal trainer, I like to arrive early at the gym to get on the elliptical machine for 15 or 20 minutes. That way, I'm 100% ready to go once it's time to put in the work with the weights. Interestingly enough, by putting in 12-plus hour workdays, I'm often on my feet in "go!-go!-go!" mode, which, combined with the stress that comes from making a living in B.C.'s volatile forest industry, keeps my heart rate up!

THAT ALL SOUNDS LIKE A LOT TO HANDLE.

I like the pace. Actually, I like "pace," period! I like getting up at 5:30 a.m., doing a bunch of work, then switching over to interview someone for my podcast, *On the Brink*. It's always been the way I've operated. I like—no, I *need*—to be busy. But I'm not a fanatic.

There's something that we haven't talked much about, but it's arguably as important as diet, nutrition, exercise—all the things we need to do to reach our ultimate goal, which is not just to avoid being chronically ill, but to be powerfully part of the world around us, even as we age into our 90s, 100s, and beyond.

That thing is being able to let go of rigidity. We need to be flexible. We need to be gentle with ourselves when we occasionally fail to achieve our goals, whether that's eating well or exercising regularly.

That's where my "80/20 Rule" comes in.

WAIT, DIDN'T YOU MENTION THIS EARLIER? CAN YOU GO OVER IT AGAIN?

Absolutely. Basically, you should aim to "do the right thing" 80% of the time. The other 20%? You can chalk it up to being human. When I say, "I don't eat red meat"—and I don't—I'm not going to completely rule out eating it. When I say, "I don't eat dairy," I'm not going to beat myself up about having an ounce or two of premium Dutch gouda. If a restaurant finishes my sole amandine off with a generous bit of butter, I'm not going to send it back to the kitchen. It's just common sense: a too-strict diet is often impossible to follow, and if you "fall off the wagon" it's damned difficult to get back on it.

It's easier if your partner is on board, too. My wife, Sharon, is extremely health-conscious. While I do eat a limited amount of meat—chicken and fish, usually—she's totally vegetarian. That works for her. I like to cut myself a bit of slack! And 80/20 flexibility has another spinoff effect. Since you're giving yourself an "escape valve" by letting go of toxic self-judgement, you can better maintain a positive mindset. And guess what? They're discovering that positivity is also critical to healthy ageing.

REALLY? HOW DOES THAT WORK?

In 2002, a multi-decades study of 660 people came out. It showed that the people who felt positively about ageing lived, on average, 7.5 years longer than those who had a negative perception. More recently, it's become clear that having a positive mindset about getting older is associated with lower blood pressure and less dementia risk.

Oh, and the other important tidbit? Positive people are more likely to exercise, which, of course, will help them live longer and feel better, which then translates into even more positivity, which of course…

Again, you see how this works. Everything is linked!

WHAT ELSE CAN HELP US LIVE LONGER, BETTER?

Sleep, for one. The vital importance of a good night's sleep seems almost cliché, but for so many of us it's easier said than done. We all know what we're supposed to do: limit screen time before bed, don't drink alcohol within a few hours of going to bed, don't exercise too soon before hitting the sack, et cetera. Although it may seem counterintuitive, sleep can help you maintain a healthy weight. Plus, swapping out sitting for sleeping—in other words, trading half an hour of couch-potato time for actual sleep—has been proven to improve attitude. You now know where that leads us!

We're finding out that sleep is a much more critical factor in our healthquest than we used to believe. A 2019 report in the journal Healthcare summed it up well:

> *Globally, insufficient sleep is prevalent across various age groups, [and is] considered to be a public health epidemic that is often unrecognized, under-reported, and [one] that has rather high economic costs…Insufficient sleep leads to the derailment of body systems, leading to increased incidences of cardiovascular morbidity, increased chances of diabetes mellitus, obesity, derailment of cognitive functions, vehicular accidents, and increased accidents at workplaces.*

Getting enough quality sleep is something that I've always intuitively known was critical. I believe that in terms of overall impact, sleep may well be the number-one area of importance—even when you consider diet and exercise. And I don't think people give it nearly as much weight as it deserves. I'd suggest that seven to nine hours a night is what everyone should be aiming for. But it's not just the number of hours spent sleeping that's critical.

There are two phases of sleep we need: one, deep sleep, and two, rapid eye movement, or REM, sleep. Both are critical to achieving and maintaining good physical and mental health, and when you get each type of sleep is also important. Deep sleep happens sooner, and it's best if this occurs before midnight, during the first sleep cycle. REM, on the other hand, occurs later—often between 1 and 4 a.m. So if you want to ensure the best sleep possible, you should probably make certain that you hit the hay earlier rather than later to get the maximum benefits of a good night's sleep.

ANY OTHER AREAS WE SHOULD KNOW ABOUT?

As any yoga aficionado will tell you, another overlooked area of fitness is balance. Poor balance and body control can lead to falls, which, as we've seen, can lead to very serious complications—especially if they require a hospital stay for, say, a broken hip. Here's a test to let you know where you stand, so to speak.

Stand with your feet together, then, with your hands on your hips, raise your left or right foot off the floor. How long can you balance? Once you've done it with your eyes open, try it again with your eyes closed, as this is a component of all major balance tests.

Depending on how old you are, this is what you should be able to do:

- 18-39 years-old: 43 seconds with eyes open, 15 with eyes closed.

- 40-49 years-old: 40 seconds with eyes open, 13 with eyes closed
- 50-59 years-old: 37 seconds with eyes open, 8 with eyes closed
- 60-69 years-old: 26.9 seconds with eyes open, 4 with eyes closed
- 70-79 years-old: 18.3 seconds with eyes open, 3 with eyes closed
- 80-99 years-old: 5.6 seconds with eyes open, 1.5 with eyes closed

I'm happy to say that I have no trouble at all with this test! Plus, with my eyes open, I could hold this pose for several minutes.

I'VE GOT TO SAY, MY BALANCE IS NOT GREAT. SO WHAT ARE THE IMPLICATIONS?

If you're almost toppling over immediately, it could be a sign that something is wrong. But if you're significantly outside the average for your age group, you probably need to work on your stability. There are balance boards and other mechanisms that can help; you should only attempt them with an exercise partner or a personal trainer. But just trying to stand on one leg and increasing the time you can do this is a great way to train.

For me, though, one of the most important longevity strategies I use has very little to do with physical fitness, at least on the surface.

WHAT'S THE STRATEGY?

I don't even know if I can call it that. It's actually a mindset, and it's one more thing that, in my opinion, you should avoid almost at all costs. It can send you spiralling downward quickly and inexorably, and the terrifying thing is that almost everyone is looking forward to it.

We plan for it. We dream about it. We fantasize what it will be like. We create communities based on this toxic premise. Entire businesses rely on our willingness to embrace it. We spend large chunks of our lives preparing for it, and the most insidious thing is that even when we finally achieve it, we don't understand that, in many cases, it's hastening our own deaths. In my opinion, it's one of the worst things you can do if you want to live a long and healthy life.

DON'T KEEP US IN SUSPENSE. WHAT IS IT?

Retiring.

WHAT? I MEAN, FOR MOST OF US, ISN'T THAT WHAT WE'RE AIMING FOR?

It is. And in my opinion, it is one of the worst things you can do if you want to live a long and healthy life. It's not just me who thinks this. But first, a bit of background. How do you think we decided on a "retirement age"? This magic number which, once you hit it, means it's all naps and nine-irons?

I HAVE NO IDEA.

According to *The New York Times*, you can probably trace it back to Germany in the late 1800s. Socialism was on the rise, you see, and the German chancellor at the time, Otto von Bismarck, had to do something to counteract this rising movement. He chose to offer Germans what had never been offered before: a retirement benefit that kicked in when you reached the age of 70.

THAT SOUNDS LIKE A SOLID, PROGRESSIVE PLAN.

Yes and no. See, back then the average life expectancy in Germany was only around 40 years. So in a sense it was a pie-in-the-sky ideal that was designed to not benefit the vast majority of Germans. It was rolled back to 65 a couple of years into the First World War. Later, other countries adopted the magic 65 number, although some are now trying to adjust it upwards. France, for example, wants to raise the retirement age by a couple of years. Unsurprisingly, this didn't go down too well with a population that has revolution in its foundational DNA.

What this means is that the age at which someone is considered old enough to retire is deeply rooted in the norms of the late 1800s through the mid-1900s. It is a relic. Yet so many of us invest in the prospect of not working and being supported modestly once we hit the age of 65, even though most of us still have productive years left.

It's a travesty. It's bad for you. And it's bad for society.

THOSE ARE TWO SEPARATE ISSUES, AREN'T THEY?

Correct. Let's take a look at how retirement affects you on a personal basis first.

The thing is, even though you start to lose brain volume in your 40s, most people remain fully cognitively functional well into their 70s and, increasingly, beyond. Studies have shown that cognitive and physical decline go hand in hand with retirement. A 2016 study published in the *Journal of Epidemiology and Community Health* tracked almost 3,000 participants over the course of nearly two decades. During that period, around 500 died.

But here's the kicker.

Those who died were almost equally divided into two subgroups: healthy and unhealthy. In the healthy group, delaying retirement by just one year made a big difference: the study's authors noted, "Among healthy retirees, a 1-year older age at retirement was associated with an 11% lower risk of all-cause mortality…independent of a wide range of sociodemographic, lifestyle and health confounders." Equally interesting: the unhealthy group also lived longer if they postponed retirement. The researchers' conclusion? "Early retirement may be a risk factor for mortality and prolonged working life may provide survival benefits among US adults."

THAT'S JUST ONE STUDY, THOUGH, ISN'T IT?

Other studies have shown similar outcomes. Again, it comes down to the fact that "65" is an arbitrary number that has never had any real relationship to how long our productive lives could be. I firmly believe that people need a reason to get up in the morning. They need to be useful and productive. They need to have a reason for being that extends beyond the 18th hole.

I'm almost in my mid-80s. I could slow down. I don't have to put in "five-to-nine" days. But I enjoy it. I am challenged, every day. I am working with people I like and admire. I am exploring new fields: how many 80-year-olds do you know who have thrown themselves into podcasting? Writing excites me. New ideas excite me. Doing stuff excites me. Taking on new challenges excites me. Being passionate—about life, about what we can achieve—now that *really* excites me. And in my opinion, it also sustains me.

HOW SO?

Again, there are numerous studies that show how keeping your mind working can help guard against cognitive decline. It translates into a positive attitude that, we've already shown, is also key to living a long and productive life. All of this circles back to my personal credo: attitude, passion, and work ethic. This credo is something to hold onto throughout your life, and it's not just a way to climb the career ladder. It's my belief that this combination will not only guarantee that you'll succeed in life, but by embracing it you will *extend* your life. You'll be happier and, as a result, healthier.

And then, of course, there's the impact that an ageing population will have on society. A 2006 study concludes, "Retiring at a later age may lessen or postpone poor health outcomes for older adults, raise well-being, and reduce the utilization of health care services, particularly acute care."

In the 2021 census there were more than 850,000 Canadians over the age of 85. Did you know that that's *twice* as many as we recorded in 2001? In just two decades, there has been a massive change in this demographic. Now, some of that is about the boomer wave rather than longevity gains: there are many more people entering this period of life than there were in 2001.

HIGHLIGHTS

OVER 861,000 PEOPLE
aged 85 and older were counted in the 2021 Census, more than twice the number observed in the 2001 Census.

THE POPULATION AGED 85
and older is one of the fastest-growing age groups, with a 12% increase from 2016. Currently, 2.3% of the population is aged 85 and older.

WHILE THE COVID-19 PANDEMIC claimed many lives among the oldest Canadians, this population continued to grow rapidly.

OVER THE NEXT 25 YEARS (by 2046), the population aged 85 and older could triple to almost 2.5 million people.

OVER 9,500 CENTENARIANS are now living in Canada — a 16% increase from 2016. Centenarians represent 0.03% of the Canadian population.

WHILE WOMEN STILL outnumber men, the ratio of women to men among people aged 85 and older is decreasing.

AS A SIGNIFICANT PROPORTION of people aged 85 and older have activity limitations or health-related issues, more than one-quarter live in a collective dwelling, such as a nursing care facility, long-term care facility or seniors' residence. This proportion increases with age.

MUCH LIKE YOUNG ADULTS, older seniors are also living downtown: in three-fifths of the country's large urban centres, there is a higher percentage of people aged 85 and older living in the downtown core than in the large urban centre as a whole. Downtown areas tend to have more services and amenities, such as hospitals, long-term care and other housing types better adapted to the specific needs of older populations.

AS MORE SENIORS ARE LIVING to 85 and beyond, an increasing number of individuals will face limitations and long-term health challenges. This will put increasing pressure on all levels of government to ensure adequate support, in areas such as housing, health care and home care, as well as transportation, among other things.

Source: Statistics Canada, 2022.

Regardless, we are witnessing the slow-motion progression of this demographic as it moves through time like an animal being digested by a boa constrictor!

There are implications for all of us. We can look at this development—

and the increase in life expectancy in general—in one of two ways.

WHICH ARE?

We can view it negatively, as a looming problem that has the potential to drain our collective resources: *How can we afford all these old people?* Or we can reframe it positively, and instead look at them as a huge reservoir of collective talent, wisdom, and experience that has the ability to radically restructure the way we live today. You can guess where I fall on this.

Here's my vision. I see a future where people regularly live robustly until they're 100 years old or older. These people aren't warehoused in hospitals or sheltering behind the walls of a gated community, trudging around aimlessly or, if they're able, playing shuffleboard. Instead, I see the collective energy of people who are pivotal to the success of society. They are providing business advice or negotiating contracts. They are part of a volunteer brigade, doing anything from cleaning up oil spills on the world's beaches to providing childcare support for a younger generation.

In a way, I see a future for our senior citizens that borrows much from the way our Indigenous peoples treat the older and wiser among their community: as Elders to be respected and learned from, for their many years of experience and the wisdom and perspective that can accompany a long and relevant life.

They—"we," actually, since at the time of this writing I'm 83—will keep mentally and physically active. We will share our cumulative life experience with the people of younger generations, thereby enriching and empowering not only ourselves but also those who come after us. We will live vibrantly and drink deeply of all that life has to offer us.

We will not be denied.

SECTION THREE

LOOKING AHEAD

CHAPTER SEVEN

THE FUTURE ISN'T WHAT IT USED TO BE

In many countries, healthcare delivery is broken. Intervening in illnesses like cancer and heart disease is prohibitively expensive, but it's the backbone of healthcare systems that prioritize intervention over prevention. So what's the best way forward? Are any countries doing it right? Would knowing more about what's good for us help produce better outcomes? What advances can we look forward to in the coming years? Is a tailored personalized healthcare approach the way of the future?

SO...IS THIS WHERE YOU DUST OFF THE CRYSTAL BALL?

I'm not sure I have one kicking around! But you can't talk about longevity without looking at it within a broader context. And a major part of that context is the issue of healthcare systems.

WHAT'S THE ISSUE?

There are several, actually. Let's zoom out and look at the big picture first. One thing that most healthcare systems share, almost regardless of which country you live in, is that they're highly reactive.

THAT DOESN'T SOUND LIKE A BAD THING.

Dig a little deeper, and you'll understand that it is. Let's play a little word game. What's the opposite of reactive? Obviously, it's *proactive.* And that's the gist of the problem—or at least one facet of it.

We've raised this before: our healthcare systems are generally designed around intervention, not prevention. The system is set up to kick in once a problem has already become a problem—in some cases, an unsolvable one. It reacts to diagnosis.

For example, if you've got diabetes, the interventions occur only once you pass a certain diagnostic threshold. But you may have been hovering around that threshold for months, years, or even decades before your numbers finally triggered the system to step in and try to solve your issue—or, as is usually the case with diabetes, manage it.

By the time this happens, you may already be on the way to losing a limb. Before you get there, though, you'll spend your time pricking your finger and measuring your blood glucose levels, hoping that the medication designed to keep the more pernicious effects of the disease at bay are helping. You're now fully invested in the reactive efficacy of the system. Lifestyle changes, while helpful, are probably no longer a curative option.

But it's possible that they *would have been.*

And it's this emphasis on being "reactive" rather than "proactive" that adds so much expense to healthcare delivery. Not to mention the human misery that many of these chronic "diseases of ageing" can bring. At this point, you're at the mercy of whatever system your country has chosen. Your life could very well depend on it.

> **We need to structure a different way of providing health care, one that isn't so reliant on getting everybody into a hospital after a medical crisis has occurred. We need prevention over intervention.**
>
> —JOHN BRINK

GOOD THING I LIVE IN CANADA, THEN.

Yes, that could be said: relatively speaking, Canada does better than many other countries in terms of healthcare outcomes. But Canadians don't get to be smug here.

A recent comparative ranking by the Commonwealth Fund, a respected U.S.-based healthcare research and advocacy organization, analyzed the healthcare systems of 11 western industrialized nations, including Canada and the United States. They ranked each system based on the following criteria: access to care, the process itself, administrative efficiency, equity, and actual outcomes. Of those 11 countries, Canada was ranked 10th. So much for smugness.

WHERE DID THE U.S. RANK?

The U.S. was dead last in a field that also included Norway, the

Netherlands, Australia, the UK, New Zealand, Germany, Sweden, France, and Switzerland. While Canada's performance fell somewhere between disappointing and shocking, it was in the ballpark of the other countries. However, the U.S. was in a category of its own. In fact, it did so badly that the researchers had to leave it out of the survey average because it was skewing the numbers for other countries.

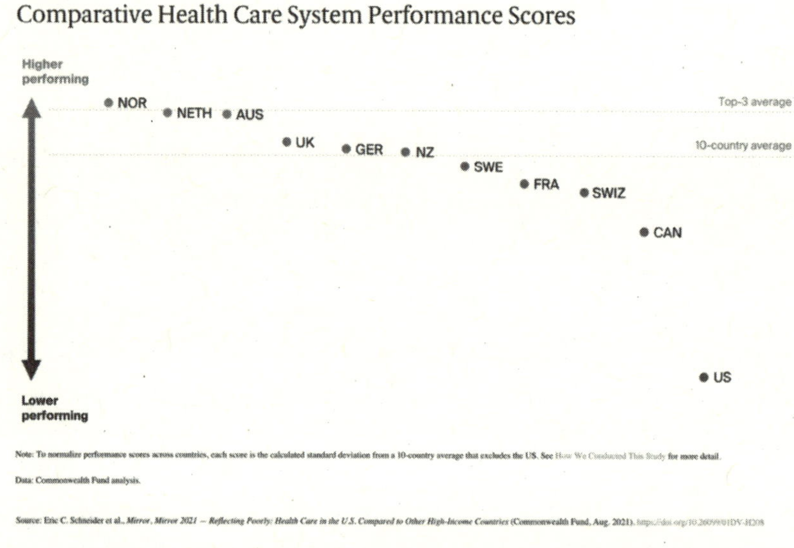

Comparative Healthcare Systems 2021 - Commonwealth Fund

Of all the countries listed in the chart, the U.S., while spending the most on health care—18.3% of their gross domestic product—gets the least back on its investment. Compared to the other nations in the study, the U.S. basically falls off a cliff.

BUT YOU ALWAYS HEAR OF CANADIANS WHO CAN'T ACCESS THEIR OWN SYSTEM MAKING THE TREK TO THE UNITED STATES TO RECEIVE TREATMENT. HOW DOES THAT SQUARE WITH THIS CHART?

You're right. And the stories can be heartbreaking. Because Canadian treatment is sort of "doled out"— each province's Ministry of Health creates its own treatment guidelines—you often hear of people who have exhausted their options in their home province and have instead sought procedures in the U.S. These could be experimental surgeries, for example, that aren't yet be covered in Canada but are offered down south. For a price, of course.

In 2023, I was struck by the story of Allison Ducluzeau, a real-estate agent who lives a hop, skip, and a jump from me on Vancouver Island. Allison had been diagnosed with Stage 4 abdominal cancer. Her family doctor proposed an innovative procedure, but when Allison went to see a colorectal surgeon, she received some startling news. According to the *Victoria*

> **Of the 11 countries included in the Commonwealth Fund study...the United States spends by far the most on healthcare—18.3% of its gross domestic product (GDP). But Americans also get by far the least return on their investment. The U.S. healthcare system finished 11th out of 11 in the rankings, and the results show it was a very distant 11th place. In fact, the United States finished so far behind 10th-place Canada that it had to be excluded from the survey average because it skewed the numbers for the other countries.**
>
> —ROSS UNIVERSITY SCHOOL OF MEDICINE

Times-Colonist, she was told that "she was not a candidate for surgery, that IV chemotherapy would not likely be effective, and she would not be referred" for the procedure. The surgeon told her that she had between two months and two years to live—and that she should "get her affairs in order."

Instead, she arranged to have the procedure done at a Baltimore, Maryland, hospital. Apparently, it went well, because "a month later, she was back at work." I'm sure Allison has no qualms about paying the CAD $200,000 cost, since it at least gave her a fighting chance at continuing her life.

The lesson is that if you can afford it, the U.S. system works well. That said, when you factor overall outcomes into the mix, it underperforms many other countries overall.

HOW DO YOU KNOW THIS?

It's easily accessible data, but one of the better comparative tools is provided by the NationMaster website. The site a clearinghouse for statistics compiled from a wide array of reputable international organizations—UNESCO, WHO, the World Bank, the OECD, and many others. You can view the stats, which include many different categories, as a nation-by-nation ranking or you can break out specific countries and compare various aspects of each.

That's what I used it for: a comparison of the U.S. and Canada when it comes to the healthcare system, health, and longevity.

AND WHAT DID YOU FIND?

Canada's publicly funded system comes out ahead in many areas. Life expectancy? Overall, Canadians live three years longer. Americans are twice as likely to be obese. Even abortion rates in the U.S. are higher, which surprised me, considering the politics. In fact, they're much higher: in the U.S., there are 4.17 abortions per 100 people, while in Canada there are 2.23. Cancer rates are roughly equal. Canada has a positive edge in heart disease, which may result from America's higher obesity rates. But the U.S. bested Canada when it came to waiting times: no big surprise there.

I've gotten some expert insight into how the two systems differ from health economist Dr. Peter Berman, Professor Emeritus of Population and Public Health at the University of British Columbia. Before coming to UBC, he spent around 25 years at Harvard's T.H. Chan's School of Public Health. Peter is American but knows both healthcare systems intimately. Clearly he's a great resource for this kind of comparison.

SO WHAT'S HIS TAKE?

He says that from the outset, the Canadian system was "explicitly designed as a medical care system," which means it was set up to provide "medically necessary services." In other words, it is pretty much resigned to being an interventionist system, intended to respond and then intervene *after* a problem has occurred.

AGAIN, THAT DOESN'T SOUND TOO BAD.

The issue is that it leaves a lot of healthcare options on the table. Berman points out, "Things like physical therapy or physical activity, improvements to diet and nutrition, these are not explicitly covered as part of medically necessary services in many situations. You have a system that essentially focuses on medical intervention and doesn't explicitly consider some of the other things that might reduce the need for medical intervention or the intensity of medical intervention."

The overlooked options he's talking about are, of course, often preventative. And they often fall through the cracks of this publicly financed healthcare system.

What's the result? Canadians can face high out-of-pocket spending for preventative actions and services that could be health-improving. Berman says, "The question that comes up is: Is this a negative feedback loop that's built into the system? Insufficient support for health-improving activities and a strong incentive to increase the use of medical interventions, which are costly?"

You see the conundrum.

I THINK SO. OUR RELIANCE ON MORE COSTLY MEDICAL CARE IS KIND OF BAKED INTO THE SYSTEM.

Precisely! Measures that could maintain, improve, or even prevent the onset of certain medical issues are often not there. The way the publicly funded system works is often after-the-fact, when there's a problem that *requires* intervention.

And that's an issue. You have a reactive system that, because of mandate and cost, focuses on fixing what has already happened, rather than on preventing what might occur. A reactive or interventionist approach might help you live longer—heart surgery, for example, might be able to extend someone's life—but it may not guarantee that you live longer and healthier. Again, it's about living *well* for longer!

The system is like a huge ocean liner, and it's very hard to turn an ocean liner around. That's especially the case when the current healthcare guarantees—timely, excellent care with equal access for all—aren't being completely fulfilled.

ARE ANY COUNTRIES DOING THIS RIGHT?

Many people point to the Nordic countries as examples. In 2023, Peter

> **You cannot imagine what you're going to see over the next 30 years. The pace of advancement is in an exponential phase right now.**
>
> — BARNEY GRAHAM, IMMUNOLOGIST AND CENTRAL FIGURE IN THE DEVELOPMENT OF MRNA VACCINES

Berman went to a meeting where people were talking about Finland's exploration of ways to integrate medical and social care. The idea was that conventional medical care would be augmented by in-home care and other areas normally overseen by, say, social workers or counsellors. Both types of service would be paid for by the same system, and they would be managed in an integrated way.

Some provinces in Canada are experimenting with similar approaches—for example, testing out "team-based care," or "primary care networks," where healthcare is delivered as part of an integrated system that includes physical therapists, speech-language pathologists, nutritionists and so on as part of a collective, unified approach. But there are barriers to the widespread adoption of this kind of system.

WHAT KIND OF BARRIERS?

Take British Columbia, for instance, which pays its primary-care doctors every time they see a patient. This means the province pays the family doctors on a fee-for-service basis. If they are going to have primary-care *networks*, how is that team going to be paid? Will the cost of additional services ultimately come out of the doctors' pockets? Or will it be in addition to what the doctor is already being paid? There is only so much money to go around.

This brings up another important point: in British Columbia, and elsewhere, there is a serious shortage of family doctors. As a result, people are forced to go to walk-in clinics for primary healthcare services. There, often after sitting in a waiting room for an unacceptable length of time, they'll likely be seen by a physician who has never seen them before and may never see them again. This is a serious issue, maybe the most serious one we're currently facing.

SO WHAT DO WE DO?

The difficulty is justifying the long game. But Peter Berman thinks that focusing on prevention strategies that fall outside the current system could go a long way. Even making improvements in nutrition—reducing meat-based diets, for example—and focusing on getting people to exercise more would pay off in the future. He thinks it could even help extend our healthspans: "Clearly, if one started to pay for more of the health-improving activities that are not medical care, this might help," he says. "The argument that many public-health people, including me, will give is that we need to carve out explicit space for these things to be invested in. If that means less for medical care, maybe that's the price we have to pay."

But as I've said, there's only a certain amount of money available. To incorporate, say, team-based care, you'll have to rob Peter to pay Paul. You see the difficulties? Big ship. Very hard to turn.

WHAT ABOUT EDUCATION? IS THERE A ROLE FOR, SAY, THE SCHOOL SYSTEM HERE? OR MAYBE THE CHILDCARE SYSTEM?

That's a very good point. There's evidence that accessing early childhood education helps prime the pump for future success, and it even benefits the parents, too: it frees them up to pursue more education, leading to higher income levels and, predictably, better health outcomes for themselves and their children.

As for the school system? I absolutely believe that there is a role to be played here, and that schools should be involved in health education as early as possible. Take nutrition. You'd think it would be a very easy thing to drill it into kids' heads that some foods and preparation methods are healthy for you and others are not. But like with so much of the news we get today, there is an enormous amount of misinformation. Disinformation, too.

And this is where things can really go off the rails. We're absolutely bombarded with health information and "breakthroughs" on a daily basis. It can be a full-time job just to wade through the junk.

SORRY IN ADVANCE FOR THE PUN, BUT THAT SEEMS TO PUT THE ONUS, WELL, "ON US."

You're right! It's up to you to make yourself the centre of your own health care. Let's get real: even if you factor out Covid-19, the healthcare systems of most western countries have been in a precarious state for years. This is a universal problem. Health care is costly, especially when your entire system is geared towards a reactive, interventionist approach.

You may be too young to remember this, but at one time, even here in Canada, if you got sick you could call your doctor and they would come to your home to assess and treat you. Imagine that! But those days are gone.

Instead, we have a system where, as we've noted, you might now count yourself lucky to even have a family doctor. If you do, you often have to book well in advance to get just a few minutes with them—and even then, you may have to instead settle for discussing your issue with someone you've never met before, much like the walk-in clinic experience. You may be seen by a locum, or maybe a nurse practitioner: we're increasingly relying on the latter to shoulder some of the diagnostic responsibility that, up until now, has been jealously guarded by physicians.

The point I'm making is that the landscape has changed greatly. The family doctor as the centre of your healthcare world is shifting rapidly. And that has massive implications for us all.

WHAT KIND OF IMPLICATIONS?

For one, because patient–family doctor interactions are becoming shorter and less involved, someone has to pick up the slack, even beyond nurse practitioners or, for example, naturopathic physicians. And that someone might have to be you.

> **We have much to look forward to in the years ahead. Those years will be miraculous, exciting, filled with all manner of awe-inspiring discoveries. All of it points to a fabulous potential: living in good health beyond 100 years of age will soon become the rule, not the exception.**
>
> —JOHN BRINK

There is no way around this reality: one of the underlying issues of Canada's so-called "single-payer system"—where the money comes from a single source, the federal government—is that it includes the promise that every Canadian, rich or poor or in between, is guaranteed equal access to medical care. On one level, this is great. It prevents the kind of problems we see in the U.S., where the leading cause of personal bankruptcy is medical debt. Factor in that almost 50% of their population has at some point decided to forgo or delay medical care because of the prohibitive cost, and you can see a clear downside to their approach.

So again, their system works well, but not for everyone and certainly not all of the time. But Canada has a different issue. When you adopt the mantra of universality, as we have, and you don't have the funds to completely deliver, what do you think happens?

I'M NOT SURE. WHAT'S YOUR TAKE?

You get universal care, but that care can be mediocre. Certain procedures that fall outside the accepted norms might not be offered. Sometimes you'll wait months before you see a specialist, and then months more before getting your problem addressed. So in some ways you establish a baseline mediocrity, neither excellent nor poor, and that's where the Canadian healthcare bar is set. As Canadians, we have dovetailed our expectations with this.

And let's be clear about what "universality" really is: if you have the means, anyone who wants to jump the healthcare queue can do it. You're only a plane ride away from accessing the U.S. healthcare system. That's what some Canadians have decided to do. Nothing prevents them from doing it.

YOU'RE ARGUING FOR PRIVATIZED HEALTHCARE, THEN?

Don't get me wrong. I'm not advocating for an American-style system, where some people get white-glove service and others get poor treatment or none. And look, the reality is that two out of three Canadians carry some type of additional healthcare insurance—like Blue Cross, for example—which to varying degrees covers everything from physiotherapy and rehabilitation work to eyewear, dental care, and prescription drugs. All of these usually fall outside of normal Canadian Medicare coverage. (Some prescription drugs will also be covered under a new national scheme when it's implemented.) But my point is that for all intents and purposes, the majority of Canadians already avail themselves of some version of "privatized" care.

SO WHAT DO WE DO? THROW UP OUR HANDS AND RESIGN OURSELVES TO WHAT WE HAVE?

No, what I'm saying is that there are alternative routes we as a society must explore, some of which could cost us now but pay off later. I know that's a difficult concept. Trust me: I'm an entrepreneur. It's always painful to have to spend now to save later. But that's exactly what we need to do. We must look at ways to improve the healthcare system. In business parlance, we need to reap superior ROI.

SORRY, "ROI"?

That stands for "Return on Investment." In other words, we need to get better healthcare returns. More bang for the buck. And we need to do it by switching our focus from being reactive to being proactive. We need to structure a different way of providing healthcare, one that isn't so reliant on getting everybody into a hospital after a medical crisis has occurred. I know this is becoming a refrain, but we need prevention over intervention. Only in this way can we afford to continue to treat people equally while at the same time extending the healthspan of Canadians.

As a nation, we need to take a long, hard look at the way healthcare is delivered in Canada. There are many routes worth testing. For example, restructuring how primary-care doctors are paid and rolling their expertise into patient-care networks in order to treat the whole person, rather than just an ailing part, could pay dividends in the future. It would be difficult, but not impossible.

I'm no expert, but I'm sure there are many options in addition to creating team-based care. However, it seems to me that the real returns will go hand in hand with prevention. To say it once again, prevention trumps intervention. Every. Single. Time.

ARE THERE ANY ECONOMIC MODELS THAT PROVE THIS? THAT INVESTING IN PREVENTATIVE MEASURES WILL PAY OFF?

Well, just off the top of my head, stop-smoking campaigns have caused lung cancer deaths to fall off precipitously, saving billions in treatment and hospitalization costs worldwide. The same could potentially happen with obesity, which the WHO has called a global epidemic. The OECD has assessed the return on investment of obesity-reduction in terms of its overall economic impact.

WHAT DID THEY FIND?

For every dollar invested, we'd be getting back $5.60 in return. I'll take those returns any day. A similar situation occurs when we look at substance abuse. According to one California cost-benefit analysis published in 2006, "On average, substance abuse treatment costs $1,583 and is associated with a monetary benefit to society of $11,487, representing a greater than 7:1 ratio of benefits to costs. These benefits were primarily because of reduced costs of crime and increased employment earnings."

Again, that's a great ROI, if all you want to do is look at it in stark economic terms. But the human suffering that is alleviated? What an extraordinary return that is. Immeasurable, in every sense.

SO WHAT'S YOUR PRESCRIPTION FOR A BETTER HEALTHCARE SYSTEM? JUST PREVENTION?

Prevention has to be the cornerstone, no question. And as we've talked about, merging conventional primary care into a team situation, where the family physician is one of several health professionals who can be assigned to treat someone, well, that would also be progress. Using nurse practitioners on a greater scale would certainly help, as would ensuring that naturopathic doctors were involved in the treatment cycle. In my view, this would be especially effective for augmenting a preventative approach, since the profession itself basically exists to further prevention, not intervention.

Another area that needs to be expanded is personalized health care.

WAIT A MINUTE: ISN'T ALL HEALTH CARE "PERSONALIZED"?

It is—just not personalized enough. The reason behind this is that the clinical trials that form the basis for evidence-based medicine—trials that have only been around since the late 1940s, by the way—are structured to take personalized information from individual participants and average it out to arrive at a baseline. In the research world, this is called "adjusting for individual differences," and it does just that: it literally erases any individual person's results from the study's conclusions!

Even though researchers need to adjust for individual differences to draw impartial and generally applicable conclusions, doing this has serious implications for how we design health care. For one, it creates medications and other treatments based on their benefit to the non-existent "average" patient, while doctors see their patients on an individual basis—and, ideally, as individuals. There is a growing push within the medical community to have researchers present doctors with the more detailed results that they need. But unless and until this happens, we're stuck with the "one size fits all" paradigm, constructed to produce a round hole into which we then try to slam square pegs—

specifically, us.

Imagine if, instead, doctors and other medical professionals took a true account of each individual patient and then designed a customized prevention or treatment routine. My god, what a fantastic, and radically different, way forward!

That's why, as you know, I do a full "bumper-to-bumper" body scan every year or so. The scan inventories any physical changes that may occur, and hopefully allows me time to address them with a course of preventative measures or, if necessary, medical treatment.

Here's an issue. At one point, we were told that after a certain age, everyone should get a colonoscopy. And then, if there was any issue whatsoever—say your doctor found a benign polyp and removed it—you'd be booked back in for a follow up in five years' time. Well, guess what? After the results of certain clinical trials, that follow-up time has now been extended to…10 years. That's right: once every 10 years is what's now recommended. *Twice* as long as before.

Now, this may be just fine for most. But what if your specific combinations of genes, lifestyle, and environment conspire to make you more susceptible to colon cancer? What if, because you're embarrassed, you fudge a bit about how much alcohol you drink on the questionnaire? What if, as a unique individual, you face a unique set of risks? The way we treat people now, it's likely that the gatekeepers of the healthcare system will simply look at what the current "best practices" are and tick that box. So you'll get your follow-up colonoscopy in about a decade—if you're around.

By then, you may have become an actuarial statistic.

BUT WOULDN'T THE COST TO OFFER, I GUESS, "A LA CARTE" HEALTHCARE PREVENTION TO EVERYONE BE PROHIBITIVE?

I don't know if that's the case. Would it be similar to those studies on obesity and substance abuse? By injecting flexibility and comprehensive personal choice into our system, would this possibly pay dividends down the road? That's an argument many make, including the authors of a 2013 *HUGO* journal article calling for medicine to move to a "P4" approach: *predictive, preventative, personalized, and participatory*. Just as I am doing here, the authors point out that the most expensive form of healthcare care is interventionist care—surgery, for example. Would it not make sense to pay for testing that could tailor a healthcare plan to each person, thereby maximizing their healthspans and keeping them out of critical care for as long as possible?

Sorry, but on this score, the U.S. system at least allows you to pursue a range of options. I know that their outcomes aren't superior in most cases. But what if you aren't most cases? What if you just happen to be you, and not some statistical average?

This is why I'm in favour of being able to order and undergo any test I want. I know: because of economics, only those with Cadillac-type healthcare plans and those with money can afford to do this. Even in the U.S., where private insurance rules, many health maintenance organizations, or HMOs, will put severe caps on what types of testing and procedures they'll fund. And yes, I also know that "individual choice" doesn't make a "system." The latter implies a broad application, and that is what we're discussing, not one person being able to do exactly what that one person wants to do simply because they can afford to do it. I get it.

But this is my life, and I will avail myself of anything I can to ensure my continued good health and hopefully achieve my goal of continuing to being a productive, lively, active, and relevant person for the remainder of my time here. Which, I'm hoping, will be until 100 years old or beyond. This is what I want. Not just for me, but for everyone.

WELL, IF THAT KIND OF CUSTOMIZED TREATMENT WAS OFFERED TO EVERYONE, THEN IT *WOULD* BE A SYSTEM.

Yes, it would. And perhaps it could. If people live longer, more productive lives that are designed not to burden the healthcare system for the majority of their years, would this not make sense economically? Again, if you put it in business parlance, you would basically be amortizing healthcare costs, on a per capita basis, by extending the amortization period over more years. And because we're concentrating on extending healthspans and increasing the number of years someone could be productive, I assume that we'd be looking at a greater return on investment, or ROI.

> **There's an overextended amount of hype associated with any new medical discovery, no matter what stage of development it's in. If we believed the promise of all these 'breakthroughs,' we'd already be living in good health until we're 500! But that's obviously not the case.**
>
> —JOHN BRINK

The cost per person per year of life would go down, wouldn't it? I'm talking off the top of my head here, but it seems like this could be part of a long-term vision.

AGAIN, THOUGH, IT SOUNDS REALLY EXPENSIVE. ARE WE AS A SOCIETY PREPARED TO MAKE THIS KIND OF INVESTMENT?

Others have. It's worth looking at what they've done in Costa Rica, for example, where the concept of community health—combining primary and public health care, along with using healthcare delivery teams and decentralized healthcare networks—has substantially increased the quality and reach of healthcare, while not leading to exorbitant expense.

So much on the horizon has the potential to save us money and guarantee better, even stellar, health care. The Covid-19 pandemic was disastrous in almost every way, of course. The death toll was unbelievable, and the social costs were enormous, with people dividing into camps and exacerbating dangerous political divisions. But there were a couple of positives.

First, it showed that rapid development of effective vaccines against a potentially calamitous disease was not a pipe dream but the end game of years of research. Second, it proved that much of our life is transportable: it can be moved online in a flash. This was significant for healthcare delivery. You could be seen virtually by a physician using Zoom-type technology. It's safer—you're not sitting in a waiting room beside someone who may be contagious—and more cost-effective on a per-visit basis than a regular in-person visit. It's one way we can stretch our healthcare dollar a little further.

WHAT OTHER OPTIONS ARE THERE?

> **"If they're in good health, and are productive contributing members of society, it will work to our benefit. If they're frail and prone to the diseases of ageing, we're screwed.**
>
> —JOHN BRINK, ON THE CONTRIBUTIONS OF OLDER PEOPLE

We're entering a brave new age of diagnostics, that's for certain. A recent article in *The New York Times* said that in the Netherlands, doctors are using artificial intelligence, or AI, to scan the DNA of brain tumours while the patient is still in the operating theatre. The technology is able to diagnose the tumour's type and even subtype. Armed with this knowledge, the surgeons can better decide "how aggressively to operate"—right there, with the patient lying in front of them. Remarkable.

This is a new twist applied to the old model of care. While it holds out hope for better outcomes, which is no small thing, it's still reactive technology, since it's treating something that has already become a problem. I think where the real payout is coming will be when we focus on being proactive.

There are major initiatives underway that are mining this vein as we speak. San Diego-based Human Longevity, Inc. is currently engaged in constructing the world's largest database of genotypes and phenotypes. Right now they offer their customers whole-genome sequencing and a battery of tests that can sniff out early markers of Alzheimer's, cancer, and heart disease.

Their "100+" program combines their diagnostic-analysis technology with a team-based medical network—a giant step forward, in my opinion, and just one of many medical-research ventures that are poised on the edge of new technology. "Our battle cry is, 'Die young as late as you can,'" the company president, Dr. David Karow, was quoted as saying in *Worth* magazine.

Sound familiar?

HA! INDEED IT DOES.

This is just the beginning. A new vaccine targets interleukin 11, thought to be one of the main disease proteins found in ageing bodies. A new blood test has been able to identify 93% of 18 different cancers in Stage 1—a point where many people are completely asymptomatic—creating more time for treatment. Ozempic, which has received so much press lately, is not just potentially beneficial in treating obesity and type 2 diabetes, but may also help combat alcohol-use disorder, liver disease, cardiovascular problems, and obstructive sleep apnea. And so on.

Currently, research into stem-cell therapies "hold great promise in treating neurodegenerative diseases, cardiovascular disease, skin diseases and cancers," notes a 2021 study published in the *World Journal of Stem Cells*. One current holdup to these treatments is that we need a lot of healthy stem cells for such therapies to be effective, and as we age, we have fewer of them. But certain strategies, such as heat shock, caloric restriction, and hypoxia, or starving cells of oxygen, are currently being looked at as a way to jump-start these older stem cells. The payoff? Eventually, we could use our body's existing stem cells to treat disease.

I don't totally understand the science behind this. Have I mentioned that I'm not a doctor and not an expert? Still, it's one more reason to think that we have much to look forward to in the years ahead. Those years will be miraculous, exciting, filled with all manner of awe-inspiring discoveries. All of it points to a fabulous potential: living in good health beyond 100 years of age will soon become the rule, not the exception.

To restate the title of this chapter, "the future isn't what it used to be." In fact, it might get positively bizarre, as we'll see next.

CHAPTER EIGHT

WHO WANTS TO LIVE FOREVER?

One of the main arguments made against radical approaches to life extension is economic: Can we afford longer lives? And what's in it for future generations? At this point in time, the idea may not be academic. Some researchers and life-extension pioneers are claiming that we could live for 150, 200, even 500 years. But should we? Would we even want to? What would our social safety net look like? What would our world become?

OKAY, LET'S SAY WE'VE IMPROVED OUR HEALTHCARE SYSTEMS. PRETEND WE'RE EATING HEALTHILY, EXERCISING REGULARLY, USING PERSONALIZED AND CUTTING-EDGE TECH TO DEAL WITH ANY POTENTIAL ISSUES—AND MOST OF US CAN NOW EXPECT TO LIVE INTO OUR SECOND CENTURY. WHAT'S NEXT?

More of the same, in a way! We're now circling back to the beginning of this book. This will be the next chapter of humankind's quest to live forever, one that started thousands of years ago. With one major difference: the kind of discoveries on the horizon could make living for hundreds of years a real possibility, not just a pipe dream.

What lies ahead—healthspans of centuries, not decades—could be within our grasp, and sooner than you think.

WHAT MAKES YOU BELIEVE THIS?

It's not just me. It's a new breed of academics and scientists, some of whom are funded by a new generation of tech CEOs with unfathomably deep pockets. All are pushing the limits of what we might be able to do.

The first time I became aware of this as something more than the magical thinking of a few individuals was when I read a 2017 *New Yorker* article called "Silicon Valley's Quest to Live Forever." One scene is set at a symposium taking place in legendary TV producer Norman Lear's Los Angeles home. A room full of celebrities, from Goldie Hawn and Moby to Google co-founder Sergey Brin, mingled with scientists like Nobel Prize-winning geneticist Liz Blackburn, who fielded questions on whether taking glutathione, an antioxidant, would be a good thing. (Spoiler alert: just make sure you're eating well, Goldie.)

When the first speaker asked how many of the attendees wanted to live to the age of 200 if they remained healthy, the writer reports, "almost every hand went up."

When I began reading, I thought that this was another exercise in ego. But it was more than that. It was the kickoff for the Global Grand Challenge in Healthy Longevity, founded by the National Academy of Medicine. The impact that it created by tapping into the wealth of Silicon Valley entrepreneurs and the vanity and PR power of the Hollywood elite has continued to this day. It is definitely a "thing."

Looking back, I suppose it was the dawn of the "tech bro" biohackers we're hearing so much about today.

WHAT EXACTLY DO THEY WANT?

They've been divided them into two basic camps: "healthspanners," and "immortalists." The healthspanners want to focus on increasing our healthspans—which is exactly what we've been talking about for much of this book. The immortalists, on the other hand, want to put our energy into essentially defeating death: essentially, to devise ways to live forever.

Let's talk about the immortalists first. One of the more prominent actors in this space is the Alcor Life Extension Foundation, which has been in business since 1972. They're based in Scottsdale, Arizona, and provide cryogenic suspension service.

WHAT DOES THIS "SERVICE" INVOLVE?

In a nutshell, when you die your body will be sent as soon as possible to Alcor, where they'll preserve it at a temperature of -192° Celsius until such time as science catches up with death. At that point, they'll thaw you out, cure you of whatever killed you and, you know, you'll walk out into a changed world, blissfully unaware of whether Taylor Swift's music has stood the test of time. Hopefully you'll still have some money to live on. It costs USD $200,000 to preserve your whole body, or, if

> **The WHO says that between 2015 and 2050, the percentage of the world's population over 60 years will nearly double, from 12% to 22%. That's 426 million, a veritable tsunami of older people that some are calling a "super-ager cohort".**
>
> —JOHN BRINK

you want to save some cash, you can opt to pay USD $80,000 to cryogenically freeze only your head.

It's not entirely science fiction. I mean, we already freeze embryos to preserve them for artificial insemination down the road: why not the whole human? Or perhaps just some viable DNA, to be reconstituted later into the person to whom it originally belonged? Even if this can't realistically be done, could we use the tissue to grow healthy organs, to be used for transplants?

I know some of this sounds too strange to be true, but I find it fascinating.

ARE THERE ANY OTHER "IMMORTALISTS" THAT WE SHOULD KNOW ABOUT?

Probably the most visible person behind the "live forever" model would be Aubrey de Grey, a computer scientist-turned-gerontologist known for his longevity science at the SENS Research Foundation, a nonprofit that focuses on researching and developing "comprehensive regenerative medicine solutions for the diseases of aging," according to their website. (De Grey was forced out of the company in 2021 after he made inappropriate remarks to two female colleagues.)

De Grey told *New Yorke*r magazine, "Gerontologists have been led massively astray by looking for a root cause to aging, when it's actually that everything falls apart at the same time, because all our systems are interrelated. So we have to divide and conquer." In 2022, de Grey claimed that we were about 15 years away from cracking the code that could essentially stop death from age-related decline. But others don't buy it. For instance, de Grey's fellow biogerontologist Matt Kaeberlein says, "It's like saying, 'All we have to do to travel to another solar system is these seven things: first, accelerate your rocket to three-quarters the speed of light…'."

And then there's Bryan Johnson.

SORRY, WHO IS HE?

Johnson made his multimillions in biotechnology. Over the past few years, he has dedicated himself to, well, not dying. Since he's still alive, I suppose you can say he's been successful, at least so far.

His path is slightly different. He's using a coordinated, personalized medical-care model called Blueprint, which he funded with USD $4 million. According to *Time* magazine, Johnson "outsources every decision involving his body to a team of doctors, who use data to develop a strict health regimen to reduce what Johnson calls his 'biological age.'" Following that regimen, Johnson "takes 111 pills every day, wears a baseball cap that shoots red light into his scalp, collects his own stool samples, and sleeps with a tiny jet pack attached to his penis to monitor his nighttime erections." In 2023, he began transfusing blood from his 17-year-old son into his own body, on the theory that "young blood" might be the key to slowing or even reversing his aging. (He stopped the experiment after six sessions, as biomarkers showed no benefits whatsoever.) Johnson thinks of any act that accelerates aging—like eating a cookie or getting less than eight hours of sleep—as an "act of violence."

He's probably not a lot of fun at parties.

BUT AREN'T JOHNSON AND DE GREY A BIT OUTSIDE THE MAINSTREAM?

Correct. That's probably why they attract so much attention. But yes, you're right: although their ranks are growing, they're still outside the mainstream longevity efforts.

AREN'T THE MAJORITY OF SCIENTISTS IN THE LONGEVITY FIELD LOOKING AT WAYS TO MAKE US LIVE LONGER AND HEALTHIER? THE "HEALTHSPANNERS," I GUESS?

Again, correct. And in my opinion, this is where the tangible gains will be made. For example, there's Retro Biosciences, which was kickstarted with a USD $180 million gift from Sam Altman, the visionary guy behind OpenAI and ChatGPT. He's on the cutting edge of the artificial-intelligence revolution, and there's no way I'd bet against him. If he sees some worth in this—and there are 180 million reasons to think he does—there may be something to it.

Retro has been pretty secretive about its work, at least until fairly recently. It's concentrating on something called "autophagy"—a word that means "self-eating," the process that happens when you fast. Autophagy is thought to rid the body of damaged cells and renew blood plasma. They're also exploring "partial cell reprogramming," which tries to alter the cellular makeup of aged animals by changing them into "younger cells," according to an article published on the Bloomberg website.

DOESN'T ALL THIS HAVE A SORT OF "WE'VE SEEN ALL THIS BEFORE" FEEL TO IT? LIKE THE MIRACULOUS CANCER BREAKTHROUGHS THAT REGULARLY COME AND GO?

I know what you're saying. I agree there's a lot of hype associated with any new medical discovery, no matter what stage of development it's in. If we believed the promise of all these "breakthroughs," we'd already be living in good health until we're 500! But that's obviously not the case.

That said, though, with the kind of energy and money that's being thrown at the quest to live longer and healthier lives, it's my opinion that nothing but good will ultimately come from it. And as I've said before, I'm now planning on living even longer than I'd once hoped; in a sense, my expectations have been raised by all that's going on. I'm planning to be around for my 120th birthday party. That's a long time, no question, but as long as I'm in good health, why not?

HOW DID YOU DECIDE ON 120?

You know, I had a fantastic guest on my podcast. Her name is Angel Stewart, and she's the force of nature behind Angel's Aerial Fitness. Angel uses non-exotic pole-dancing techniques combined with circus-like equipment—aerial hoops, hammocks, that sort of thing—to promote physical fitness. She's been in business since 2008 and currently has about 160 clients and 10 staff.

Aside from the novel aspects of what she does, I loved the fact that she had set herself a goal: to live until she was 120. Before, I'd settled on 100, since it doubles as a significant milestone. But after meeting Angel, I decided I wanted to add a couple of decades too.

THAT'S ALL WELL AND GOOD, BUT—AND I HATE TO RAIN ON THE PARADE—THERE ARE NO GUARANTEES.

Of course not, and Angel knows this too. "Even if it doesn't happen, I believe I will have a better quality of life," she told me. "If everybody lived believing that the expected lifespan is 150 or 200, I think more 60-year-olds would go back to school and learn something new."

I was floored. She is a remarkable person. She's 40, as of 2024, so one-third of the way there.

BUT ARE WE EVEN READY FOR THIS, AS A SOCIETY?

We've touched on this in the previous chapter, but there will be challenges, no question. Countries are already spending a ridiculous percent of their gross domestic product on old-age pensions. In France, where they controversially tried to scale the percentage back by raising the retirement age from 62 to 64 in 2023, they spend 14.1% of GDP on pension benefits. Italy is in an even greater bind: 15.7% of their economic output goes to sustaining their pension system.

The stats are sobering. And the proportion of old people is growing faster than ever before. The WHO says that between 2015 and 2050, "the proportion of the world's population over 60 years will nearly double from 12% to 22%." That's 426 million, a veritable tsunami of older people that some are calling a "super-ager cohort." But if they're in good health, and if they're productive, contributing members of society, it will work to our benefit. If they're frail and prone to the diseases of ageing, we're screwed. That's why we need to take the necessary steps to ensure that these "super-agers" represent a net value to the economy, rather than a massive drain.

Do you want to saddle the younger generations with this kind of debt? It's hardly fair.

SO WHAT STEPS CAN WE, AS A SOCIETY, TAKE?

There's a great report from The Stanford Center on Longevity that's worth looking at. It's called the "The New Map of Life," and it tracks the 10 major steps we'll need to take to enhance the quality of longer lives. Here's a summary of their 10 steps:

1. Capitalize on "the 100-year opportunity": In other words, make sure that people can still be contributors as they age. As the report's authors put it, "Many people experience functional independence well into their 70s and 80s...The potential for longer working lives is linked more clearly to ability, desire and need, rather than chronological age."

2. Invest in future centenarians: With a longer healthspan, we can afford to extend our more carefree youthful years—to stretch out adolescence, for example. It's all about "optimizing each stage of life."

3. Line up lifespans with healthspans: no explanation required!

4. Prepare to be amazed by the future of aging: again, we've covered much of this, from adopting personalized medicine to embracing the technological miracles that will surely come to pass—sooner rather than later.

5. Treat life transitions as a feature, instead of a glitch: I love this! We need to alter our perceptions to embrace change, rather than resist it.

6. Encourage lifelong learning: Whether it's in a formal educational setting or simply giving in to your innate curiosity, learning=growth.

7. Work more years, in a more flexible way: You don't have to

put in eight-hour days if you don't need to or want to. The key is making your working life work for you—or in my case, making work and life pretty much one and the same.

8. Focus on building financial security from the outset: Since you'll be living longer, your money will need to last longer too. Financial literacy will become the hallmark of the new era.

9. Think of age diversity as being a positive for society and the economy: We need to shift our thinking, and embrace the wide variety of skills, energy, and assets that everyone, regardless of age group, can bring to the table.

10. Build longevity-ready communities: Not retirement homes but *communities*, where we all live. Built diverse environments that can keep people safe, happy, well, and involved in community. It can be done.

In effect, this is a blueprint for a better world. Hats off to Stanford on this one!

ONE MORE QUESTION BEFORE WE LEAVE THIS SUBJECT. WE'VE TALKED ABOUT THE PROMISE OF EVERLASTING LIFE. EVEN IF WE CAN ACTUALLY DO IT. . .SHOULD WE?

Oh, my. This is such a layered question. In this case, though, I'm going to circle back to that *New Yorker* article, which ended on this same note. In closing, the article quoted world-renowned geneticist Nir Barzilai, who was speaking to a group of about 300 people about longevity. He said:

> *"In nature, longevity and reproduction are exchangeable. So Choice One is, 'You are immortalized, but there is no more reproduction on Earth, no pregnancy, no first birthday, no first love'—and I go on and on and on... Choice Two is you live to be eighty-five and not one day sick, everything healthy and fine, and then one morning you just don't wake up."*
>
> *"Choice One got ten or fifteen people. Everyone else raised their hands for Choice Two."*

When it comes to the possibility of living forever, there is, upon reflection, much to lose.

CONCLUSION

AND SO, METAPHORICALLY SPEAKING, we come to the end of our journey. But really, "the end" is something that we must always have in our sights.

For me, at least, this journey does not go on indefinitely. Although immortalist ideas intrigue me, and I expect that chasing a present-day Fountain of Youth will likely pay off for all of us, I'm not an immortalist. Living forever, on a too-crowded planet with limited resources, feels like a betrayal of those not yet alive, who could inject new energy and perspective into discoveries that will propel us all forward. We are not just a collection of unconnected individuals. We must act together to ensure that the human spirit, this thread that connects us over time, space, and distance, remains strong and viable.

Rather, I'm a *healthspanner*. For me, this is a no-brainer. It straddles the divide between those who want to avoid death entirely, and the current status quo where people die too young or, perhaps worse, too old for their own good. We've already discussed what this looks like. Suffice it to say that for far too many of us, the last years of our lives are extremely difficult.

If there's one takeaway I'd love readers to get from this book, it's that we need to shrink the gap between death and decline. As I've said, I plan to live until 120, and I don't see any reason why this won't be feasible. I'm in excellent health. I'm productive and engaged—more than most 80-year-old–plus guys, that's for sure. In the past decade or so I've reinvented myself a few times. Actually, it's not "reinvention" so much as it's "extension." Writer. Podcaster. Public speaker. Philanthropist. Real-estate developer. Industry disruptor. Advisor to government on forestry policy. Provider of shipping and warehousing services—logistics. And, as always, an entrepreneur at heart.

It's a busy life, and a good life, too. Although I have no empirical evidence to support this, I feel that the way I've chosen to live enables me to live longer and better, and that I'll continue to do so well into the next decades. Again, my credo comes into play: *Attitude. Passion. Work ethic.* As I've said, it's a formula for success but also so much more. It is an integral part of a longevity strategy that could add years to your life—and life to your years.

What, then, have we learned? What goes into "living young, dying old"?

The answer isn't all that complicated. Eat well and smartly, but not too much. If you need to, take supplements to counteract deficiencies. Get a good amount of restful sleep. Don't overdo things that we know can negatively impact us: cut down on alcohol, don't smoke, and limit unhealthy, over-processed foods. Know yourself, since realizing the parameters of your own health can be the first step in addressing health issues before they become overwhelming. If a specific condition runs in your family, understand that all is not lost: it's often possible to alter your "fate" by doing the right things. That said, be judicious in what you buy into: avoid junk-science cures and pie-in-the-sky promises by marketers. Snake oil continues to be sold and consumed even today.

Exercise, the so-called "miracle drug," is key. You don't have to be a long-distance runner or, for that matter, a competitive bodybuilder to benefit: move naturally and regularly, and incorporate strength training into your routine. But don't be too rigid in your approach: cut yourself a little slack, since that can allow you to continue on your wellness path without the burden of negative self-judgement.

Finally, make yourself matter. Be a partner and friend, or a reliable family and community member. Be someone who embraces each day and makes the most of your time on earth. Choose a career you love, and continue to do it long after some arbitrary "retirement age" milestone passes. You can scale back if you need to, but remain active, involved, and relevant. This benefits you and others: don't underestimate the reservoir of wisdom and knowledge you've accumulated over time. Put it to good use: mentor someone, give a hand. Be active. Be useful. Be generous.

As you age, be exactly who you always wanted to be, but armed with the hindsight to really understand what matters. Do this and you will live robustly, vibrantly. Live young, always. Die old and content.

Thank you so much for coming along with me on this journey. I hope it's been as interesting and enlightening for you as it has been for me. I wish you many blessings, but mainly the blessing of excellent health well into the twilight of your life.

I want to close with a relevant quotation. It's not ancient wisdom. It's not from Voltaire, Benjamin Franklin, or any religious text. It is, in fact, from *Star Trek*: "Live long and prosper."

Yours in good health,

JOHN A. BRINK

John A. Brink is President and CEO of Brink Forest Products, one of the largest forestry companies in British Columbia. He is the founding President of the B.C. Council of Value-Added Wood Processors. In addition to his success in business, John is a dedicated philanthropist and long-time supporter of amateur and professional athletes. He is a nationally ranked competitive bodybuilder and rides dressage weekly with his wife, Sharon. John is a member of the Order of British Columbia and a Distinguished Toastmaster. He holds an honorary Doctor of Laws degree from the University of Northern British Columbia. John is the successful host of the On The Brink Podcast, which has accumulated over 20 million views world-wide on various streaming platforms. He lives in Prince George and North Saanich, British Columbia. John has lived his entire life with attention-deficit/hyperactivity disorder (ADHD).